# CONTENTS

D0353137

# FOREWORD

Deciding what to leave out is always the most difficult part of editing. This was particularly true while compiling this collection of Mary Raftery's columns. I worked closely with Mary for many years and her knowledge and interest in a huge range of subjects never ceased to amaze me. She had an insatiable curiosity and a strong sense of justice and this is reflected in the breadth of subjects she addressed in her opinion columns, which were published in the Irish Times every Thursday from 2003-2007.

When editing this selection I attempted to categorise the columns under headings such as health, children, the economy etc. but soon realised that so many of the columns defied classification. While each column stands alone, when taken together they present an insightful commentary about Irish society during "the boom" years.

Mary is best known for the outstanding work she did in relation to exposing the abuse of children in States of Fear (1999) and Cardinal Secrets (2002). It was important to include some of the analysis pieces she wrote at the time of the publication of the Ryan and Murphy Reports in 2009, both of which arose out of these programmes. Her analysis pieces appear at the end of this book.

And the title? "Do they think we are complete eejits?" is a phrase Mary used regularly and it is a question that comes to mind when reading many of these columns.

I would like to thank David Waddell, Sheila de Courcy and Finn Ahern for their help; also thanks to the team at the Irish Times: Michael Ruane, Denis Staunton and Angelo McGrath and a special thanks to Fintan O'Toole for all his support with this project.

**Sheila Ahern**
*Editor*

# INTRODUCTION
*Fintan O'Toole*

Mary Raftery, who died far too young in 2012, was unquestionably the most important Irish journalist of the last 30 years. The best journalists hope they might manage to reflect with reasonable accuracy the society they inhabit. Mary Raftery did that supremely well. But she was one of the very few members of the profession anywhere of whom it can be said without a hint of exaggeration that they didn't just reflect their society, they changed it.

In her case, she changed Ireland significantly and for the better. The paradox of her work is that she made the place more decent and civilised largely by showing it the indecent and uncivilised sides of itself. She was an old-fashioned optimist who believed that the truth, however frightful, makes us free. No one has ever done more to free Ireland from toxic illusions about its own sanctity.

Mary Raftery was born in Dublin in 1957, spent part of her childhood abroad (her father was a diplomat), excelled in maths, physics and music and went to UCD in 1975 to study the then almost exclusively male subject of engineering. She first appeared in The Irish Times in 1977 when its education correspondent Christina Murphy interviewed her because she had been elected as the first female full-time officer of the students' union: "Mary Raftery is 19 years old, she looks about 14 and she goes about her job in a manner which makes you think she might be 25." She never went back to finish her degree and instead began to work as a freelance journalist, first for In Dublin magazine and later for Magill. At In Dublin she wrote a famous investigation (in retrospect highly prescient of the worst excesses of the Celtic Tiger property boom) into a notorious developer, headlined "Patrick Gallagher, Property Speculator and Brat". As she recalls in a column collected here, "Patrick Gallagher had declined to be interviewed for the piece, but afterwards decided he did want to talk to me. I was summoned to a surreal evening in one of the large snugs of Ryan's in Parkgate Street, where Gallagher was ensconced with business cronies and family members. Between sessions of climbing on tables and singing loudly, he wanted to know why we had called him a brat. He wasn't a brat, he said, and wanted us to take it back. Since he then immediately burst into song again, it was difficult to take him seriously." She may have looked 14 (or perhaps 16 by then) but she was not easily intimidated.

She went to work as a television producer for RTE in 1984, and encountered the worst expectations of journalistic subservience. She was given the job of producing the 1986 Fianna Fail Ard Fheis, and in particular the speech of its then leader Charles Haughey: "I was summoned to the royal presence. Charlie shook my hand, and without speaking, clicked his fingers. The door opened, and in paraded a line of people carrying an assortment of suits, ties and shirts. 'Take her in there,' barked The Boss, 'and get her to pick out what I should wear for the speech.' … Bemused, I meekly trotted after the row of human clothes hangers. PJ Mara, the voce at the time for his Duce, pressed me for a decision. The extraordinary assumption that I, as an RTÉ journalist, was there to provide advice as to how to make the Fianna Fail leader look good on television was profoundly revealing of the party's attitude to the national broadcaster. Together with everything else in the country, they considered that they owned it." Fianna Fail, she recalls, "appeared to have cast me as some form of latter-day Leni Riefenstahl". It was a spectacularly bad piece of casting.

More to her taste was making investigative programmes for Today Tonight (later Prime Time) and the pioneering health series Check Up. It was typical of her of her tenacity and courage that, at Today Tonight, she produced the first documentary evidence of a truth that every Irish journalist knew but none could prove – that Charles Haughey was on the take. She found, in a receiver's report on Patrick Gallagher's failed property and banking empire, reference to a payment from Gallagher to Haughey. Not for the first or last time, she had to battle through legal obstacles to tell the public what she had discovered: RTÉ, as she recalls in a column collected here, "ruled that we should exclude all reference to money handed out to Haughey by Gallagher from our programme exposing the latter's fraudulent activities." From early on, Mary Raftery's career was the embodiment of Lord Northcliffe's famous definition: "news is what somebody somewhere wants to suppress; all the rest is advertising".

The other side of Mary Raftery's work, though, was evident on Check Up – her extraordinary empathy with people who were having a hard time. The programme was much tougher than health-related features tend to be, breaking taboos around areas like medical negligence. But the investigative rigour was matched by an enormous and genuine sympathy for people who were ill, vulnerable and suffering, by the ability to understand, as she puts in a column reprinted here, "how it feels to be weak, sick and helpless within a system which is profoundly dysfunctional." She may have been utterly uncompromising in holding those in power to account, but she also developed a very special ability to listen sympathetically to so-called ordinary people.

Listening, oddly enough, is not something most journalists do very well. Journalism is busy, noisy, pressured. Journalists pride themselves on their ability to get in, get the job done, get out. Mary Raftery worked under all of these pressures, yet she also developed a capacity to spend time with people who needed someone to listen to them.

Journalists are quite comfortable with the notion that news is what someone somewhere wants to suppress – it's what gives the activity its primal energy. But they're far less comfortable with the opposite: that news might also be what someone has been desperate to say, if only someone would listen. The stories of appalling abuse of children in industrial schools that became the explosive States of Fear series were not the classic stuff of investigative journalism in that they were not secret. The institutions in which the abuse occurred were not hidden – they loomed over many Irish towns. Around 170,000 children had been through those institutions and almost all of them had experienced or witnessed systematic cruelty. From time to time, some prominent people (like Father Flanagan who is the subject of one of the columns collected here) had spoken out about what was happening. There was no shortage of material or of people with stories to tell. What had been largely lacking was the capacity to listen to those stories and the courage to face down the powerful interests for whom these truths were unsayable.

We now know, from the troubles that both RTE and the BBC got themselves into in trying to tell stories of child abuse, how damnably difficult it is to combine empathy with rigour, to descend into the darkness of traumatic memories and emerge, not just with an emotional or psychological truth but with an objective, evidence-based truth that can be justified in the public world. So much has gone wrong in the broadcasting of these stories that States of Fear and Cardinal Secrets, the two key documentaries on abuse and cover-up within the Irish Catholic church now seem even more remarkable in their clarity, precision and unimpeachable accuracy. What is more remarkable still, however, is that this exemplary professionalism was at the service of the simple, instinctive emotions of compassion for people and revulsion against cruelty.

These were personal, not just professional, qualities. Mary Raftery was a very private person, but she spoke once about her memory of being a very little girl, jumping off the stairs at home into her father's arms. She would go up another step higher and jump again, completely sure that he would be there to catch her. It was an image of what every child should have: the confidence that comes from unquestioning trust.

One might speculate that this memory drove her on, that because she had emerged from her own childhood armoured with this confidence and comfort, she could not abide the thought of such trust being abused and betrayed. Once her work brought her into contact with those whose childhoods had been stolen from them, she could not and would not allow them to be abandoned again. She could not turn away from the thought of those children for whom there was no one to catch them when they fell or, worse still, who fell into the arms of cruelty, exploitation, neglect and abuse.

What made this impulse so potent, though, was Mary Raftery's unique mix of steeliness and tact. She was uncompromising in her attitude to those who had abused power but extremely sensitive to the dignity of those who had been abused. Journalistic investigations, however well-intentioned, can have the effect of re-traumatising people who have undergone horrendous experiences. Together with the editor of this collection, Sheila Ahern, Mary Raftery developed an approach to ways of telling the stories of people who had been traumatised that is of international importance because it applies to every situation in which human rights have been traduced. Central to that approach were both intelligent listening and a willingness to give people power over their own stories. Without compromising the necessary independence and scepticism of journalism, it challenged the idea that the sole responsibility of the journalist is to the viewer or reader, the consumer of the story. At the heart of her work was the idea of an even more important responsibility – to the humanity and innate value of those whose stories were being told.

The one respect in which Mary Raftery did not set the best example was in the way she built a great contribution to society on her failure to follow through on her education. She studied to be an engineer and to be a classical cellist and gave up on both. Journalism is an odd profession, where half-formed bits of oneself can somehow cohere in the act of telling a story. Both engineering and music contributed qualities that combined to make her work so formidable.

From the engineer that never was, the journalist took form, precision, structure. With her mathematical rigour, her studious meticulousness, she built great structures of narrative, in print and in television programmes. Those structures had to be extraordinarily resilient because they were tested with extreme ferocity. In retrospect, after the official State apologies and the commissions of inquiry and the eventual public acceptance of the truths she told, it is easy to say that of course she was right. But at the time the structures she built had to withstand ferocious gales of denial, outrage and personal abuse.

But that robustness would have been useless without the qualities that the would-be musician brought to her work. To be a musician requires sensitivity, an ear for nuance, the tact to know the right note at the right moment, and above all a sense of empathy. Anyone who worked with her, especially those who were hurt and wounded by cruelty and abuse, knew her genuine care for those who had been treated as the scum and refuse of the Republic. The hard anger she felt at the cruelty she encountered was always rooted in a deep tenderness for vulnerable humanity. Hers was not Jonathan Swift's "savage indignation". It was a compassionate indignation at savagery.

She knew she was dealing, not with journalistic material, but with the fragile and precious stuff of human lives and personalities. She knew that these people had been exploited and was determined, above all, not to exploit them again. She countered the corrupting effects of absolute power with kindness, decency and above all with respect.

That kindness is everywhere in these columns, written for The Irish Times between 2003 and 2009 Almost of all of them are, in one form or another, about matters of public policy – official decisions or systems or sometimes simply official ignorance and neglect – or of corporate or institutional irresponsibility. But what distinguishes them from the general run of op-ed analysis is that, time and again, they're really about what bad government or bad policies or official neglect do to real people. Only rarely do we glimpse the reality that these people are vulnerable individuals for whom Mary Raftery herself is a last hope. In the story of Bruno Hrela, who is trying to get the Vatican to give him a copy of a letter he sent 50 years earlier about his abuse in Artane industrial school, she mentions that "From time to time, Bruno phones me from London, where he has lived for many years. When he talks about Artane and his letter and the current Pope, there often comes a point where he can't continue, where he breaks down and cries. The sadness never leaves you, he says." There were many, many Brunos.

What makes these columns so compelling, long after the original occasion for their publication has passed, is that their touchstones are not statistics or abstractions but deep human emotions and impulses: sadness, grief, memory, oblivion, justice. The standard by which everything is measured in Mary Raftery's columns is the way it affects so-called ordinary lives, and especially those at the bottom of the heap – the disabled man in the sheltered workshop, the prisoner in vile conditions, the child at the mercy of a chaotic care system, the person with a mental illness stuck in a Dickensian hospital.

It is chastening to remember that all of these columns were written at a time when Ireland was boasting of  being one of the richest countries in the world, when many people seemed to have, quite literally, more money than they knew what to do with. The columns cast an acutely sceptical eye on the values of the time, not least as expressed in the Irish Times itself: "In a fashion article in this newspaper a few weeks ago featuring charity ball organisers, one said that her ideal charity event is Elton John's, with its concept of wearing as many diamonds as possible.  Another spoke of the downside of € 2,000 designer gowns – once you wear them to a ball, it's very hard to wear them again to another event. She assured us, however, that she does get two to three years out of an Armani outfit." And this madness is seen too at an official level: "'Mickey Mouse' was the term they used on Tuesday to describe the offer made to them of a new annual salary of €205,000 plus bonuses of €40,000. Faced with such a derisory offer, the Irish Hospital Consultants Association has abandoned negotiations and intends taking industrial action."

These vignettes have a certain rueful humour now, but they do reminds us that there are many different ways in which a society can lie to itself. It can choose not to know about the viciousness that lies beneath its surface or it can flaunt a deluded sense of entitlement. Dangerous ignorance can be created by over-mighty churches or over-greedy secular elites. It can manifest itself in unspeakable darkness or in crass glamour. But whatever form it takes it has seldom had a more potent enemy than Mary Raftery.

# Trust me, I'm a doctor . . .

*July 31, 2003*

Anyone going into hospital to have a baby these days could be forgiven for being seriously scared. What has emerged over the past year of the obstetric practices of Dr Michael Neary would cause even the most stoical of parents to blanch. But it is more how the medical profession has dealt with the issues raised by Dr Neary's practices which would so seriously shake the confidence of not just prospective parents, but of everyone who has any dealings with doctors in this country.

Dr Neary was last year found to be negligent by the High Court for having performed an unnecessary Caesarean hysterectomy on Alison Gough in Our Lady of Lourdes Hospital in Drogheda. Another 65 similar cases have yet to be heard by the courts. Ten complaints against Dr Neary have this week been upheld by the Medical Council, the body charged with supervising a doctor's fitness to practise medicine, and the council has struck him off the medical register.

So far, so good, you might think. However, it has taken the Medical Council 4½ years to reach this point. This is hardly the kind of prompt action which might allay the entirely justified fears of patients and attempt to repair the damage to doctor/patient relationships. It is difficult to escape the conclusion that the Medical Council, made up almost entirely of doctors, simply doesn't take very seriously the business of complaints against the profession.

It is instructive to look at some of the council's complaints statistics. Since 1999, when the current council was appointed, it has received an average of 235 complaints a year. Over 90 per cent of these were dismissed without even a hearing. Of the cases considered in 2002 (405, which included a backlog), the council decided that only 14 warranted even further consideration. In just one area, that of doctors' failure to communicate and rudeness, the council received 117 complaints during the past five years. In only a single case was even further inquiry deemed appropriate. All of this is against a background of high levels of medical litigation in this country. We are constantly admonished by the medical profession that we as a nation are far too eager to go to court if anything goes wrong with our treatment. But a startling study by the St Paul insurance company has indicated a radically different picture. It surveyed reported incidents of potential malpractice over the past five years and discovered that patients sued in only one-third of the cases examined. A fair and somewhat alarming conclusion from this is that medical negligence in Ireland is in reality a far more serious problem than we had previously thought. So rather

1

than being overly litigious and compo-crazy, as the medical profession would have it, patients actually don't sue doctors nearly enough.

Doubtless doctors would prefer that we should instead all go to the Medical Council, to have our cases adjudicated by other doctors and most likely summarily dismissed.

Even the Medical Council itself had a vague unease about its own procedures in the Neary cases. Last summer, in response to scathing criticism from Patient Focus and several of Neary's victims, the council commissioned former attorney general Harry Whelehan to review those procedures. He produced his full report to the council last June, which has so far refused to publish it. According to a report in the Irish Medical Times earlier this month, Whelehan was highly critical of the council.

He stated that some complaints against Neary were not recorded, were misfiled, were not acknowledged and were ignored. Reasonable standards are not being met and inquiries are fragmented, according to his review. He talks of a "sense of disillusionment" among those complainants whose files he reviewed. He felt it understandable that people would feel that there was "a general lack of interest in pursuing complaints", and that they were not being taken seriously.

In this context, it is not surprising that so many people who are the victims of medical negligence choose to ignore the only body in the State charged with the regulation of doctors, and instead go to court. Doctors complain that high levels of litigation can lead to the practice of defensive medicine to the detriment of patients. However, it is now clear that the responsibility for this vicious circle lies fairly and squarely with the medical profession, which clings firmly to the principle that it should continue to be allowed to regulate itself through a Medical Council structure.

Trust is a word often quoted by the medical profession - it is what we, the patients, are expected to confer on them. The Medical Council is supposed to ensure that we can be confident that our trust is justified. It is palpably obvious that the Medical Council is failing in this most fundamental task. Professional self-regulation by doctors is simply not working.

It is now incumbent on the Minister for Health and Children, Micheál Martin, to intervene urgently to create transparent and fully independent mechanisms for the hearing of complaints against doctors. What is at stake here is literally life and death.

# Restoring dignity to Magdalens

*August 21, 2003*

Exactly 10 years ago, a firm of Dublin undertakers began a mass exhumation in Drumcondra. As far as they were concerned, the papers were all in order: 133 bodies were to be dug up and ferried to Glasnevin Cemetery, where they would be cremated. It was a small burial plot, with the graves unmarked except for a few plain black crosses. Not exactly a run-of-the-mill job for the undertakers, but not that unusual either. It was only when they discovered 22 additional bodies that alarm bells began ringing. This was a burial site for Magdalens, women who had effectively been locked up for most of their lives, working for no wages in High Park convent, one of the largest and oldest Magdalen Laundries in the country.

By the early 1990s, the laundry had closed and the nuns - the Sisters of Our Lady of Charity of Refuge - were selling their land to housing developers. The nuns had gambled and lost on the stock exchange and needed cash. The snag was the graveyard for the Magdalen women who had died in their service was on the land they had sold. So the good Sisters did a deal with the developers that each would pay half the cost to clear the land of the remains. To exhume a grave, you need an exhumation licence from the Department of the Environment. The nuns were granted such a licence for 133 bodies buried at the High Park plot. The list of names they provided to the Department makes for interesting reading. Twenty-three of the women are listed under the heading "quasi-religious name" - the nuns admitted that they did not know their real names. They called them "Magdalen of St Cecilia, Magdalen of Lourdes, Magdalen of St Teresa", and so on. Another woman had only a first name. The nuns told the Department that as they had no names, death certificates for these 24 women could not be produced. The Department raised no objection, despite the fact that some of the women had died as recently as the late 1960s. The nuns also said that there were no death certs for a further 34 women. These women at least had names. But the cause and date of death for most of them are listed as "not known". Some of these women died as recently as the mid-1970s.

It is a criminal offence in this State to fail to register a death which occurs on your premises. This is normally done by a relative. In the case of the Magdalen women, it was the legal duty of the nuns to register their deaths. It would appear that for at least 58 of these women, the nuns failed to do so. And then there were the additional 22 bodies discovered by the undertakers. All work on the graves had to cease immediately, as these remains were not covered by the exhumation licence. What the Department of the Environment then did beggars belief. Rather than halting proceedings to investigate, they simply put through an additional licence to allow the nuns to remove all bodies from the graveyard. They didn't even ask if anyone knew the identities of the extra 22. All but one of the bodies were cremated, destroying any possibility of future identifications. The nuns had been informed that the cost of reburying the remains intact would be considerable, and so they went for the cheaper option.Until 20 years ago, cremation was forbidden by Catholic Church canon law. Even today it is frowned on as undesirable. Canon 1176 now "earnestly recommends that the pious custom of burial be retained". None of this cut much ice with the High Park nuns. Cremation proceeded smoothly, despite the fact that the State was fully aware that more than half the deaths of those exhumed had never been certified. The ashes were interred in a plot in Glasnevin. A headstone with a list of names now marks the grave. However, a comparison of the names and dates on that headstone and the list supplied by the nuns to the Department of the Environment is startling. Only 27 of the names and dates coincide. So either the list of names given to the Department to obtain the exhumation licence was substantially false, or the names on the Glasnevin gravestone bear little relation to the identities of those actually buried there.

Last Easter, I asked the nuns at High Park to explain all of this. They chose not to respond to any of the 19 detailed questions I put to them. Instead, earlier this week, they issued a statement claiming that the exhumation was carried out in order to provide the women with a permanent resting place. Their concern to respect the dead Magdalen women is no doubt touching. But might perhaps the Minister for Justice be concerned enough to investigate so many unexplained and unregistered deaths? And who will care enough to restore to these women the dignity of their real names - something the nuns stripped ruthlessly from them in life? It is surely the duty of the State to return some respect to these, its citizens, whom it deserted so comprehensively both in life and in death.

# Ratzinger sings an old song

*August 5, 2004*

So the Catholic Church doesn't like feminism. Well, blow me down, who would have thought it! Cardinal Ratzinger, in his letter at the weekend to bishops on Collaboration between Men and Women, goes further than the Pope himself in his hostility to feminism.

In 1995, John Paul II identified some of the demands of feminists for the liberation of women as "legitimate". But not any more, it would appear. Joseph Ratzinger has long been the most powerful cardinal in the Vatican. Head of the Congregation for the Doctrine of the Faith (formerly the Inquisition division), his pronouncements in this case carry the full authority of the Catholic Church. "The Church is called today to address certain currents of thought which are often at variance with the authentic advancement of women," he proclaims and proceeds to identify feminism as this evil which is holding women back. His message is clear: for women, feminism bad, Catholic Church good. The document identifies recent trends in relation to women as entirely negative: emphasis on subordination in order to create antagonism to men; lethal effect on families; denial of differences between the sexes; equivalence of hetero and homosexuality. All this, it says, "strengthens the idea that the liberation of women entails criticism of Sacred Scripture, which would be seen as handing on a patriarchal conception of God nourished by an essentially male-dominated culture. Second, this tendency would consider as lacking in importance and relevance the fact that the Son of God assumed human nature in its male form." And this is the key to the document: feminism is dangerous because it leads to baseless criticism of the Catholic Church as a patriarchal and male-dominated institution. According to Ratzinger, women are infinitely better ("listening, welcoming, humility, faithfulness, praise and waiting") than those feminists who make "demands for ourselves", and deny the difference between the sexes.

So let's look at this business of women being different to men. It is not a concept that the Vatican or the Church Fathers have ever had any difficulty with. In fact, throughout the centuries, they have made it very clear that the main difference is that women are inferior. The eminent German theologian Ute Ranke-Heinemann, in her wonderful book, Eunuchs for the Kingdom of Heaven, details with erudition exactly what the Church has thought about women since its earliest days. She has been condemned by the Vatican, which revoked her licence to teach theology in 1987. Quoting from a wide variety of Popes and Church Fathers, the founding theologians of Catholic moral thought, she puts together a profoundly shocking picture of pathological misogyny.

According to Church Fathers such as Augustine and Thomas Aquinas, women had "less strength of mind", were "intended for procreation", and needed greater care "because of their ready inclination to sin". Aquinas believed that women, as "nature's second intention" were a sort of defective version of the male. Man has "more perfect reason" and "stronger virtue" than woman, whose "defect in her reasoning ability", which is "also evident in children and mentally ill persons", made her unsuitable to give evidence in canon law trials. One of the most extreme of this band of clearly disturbed individuals was St Albert the Great, honoured by the current Pope some years ago on the anniversary of his birth. Albert didn't hold back: women are "inconstant", have "a faulty and defective nature", know "nothing of fidelity", engage in "lying and diabolical deceptions". According to this highly influential saint, who continues to be honoured in the Church today, "her feelings drive women towards every evil, just as reason impels man towards good".

All very interesting, you might well say, but is it relevant in today's culture? The answer is a resounding yes. Much of Cardinal Ratzinger's document is a theological analysis of the Book of Genesis, original sin, concupiscence, and virginity - concerns which were precisely those of Augustine, Thomas Aquinas and Albert. The Church Fathers perceived women as either virgin or harlot. While the harlot bit has now receded somewhat, the Ratzinger document continues to perceive the idealisation of women through the prism of Mary, as virgin before, during and after the birth of Jesus. While Cardinal Ratzinger does put a different spin on some of these aspects, there is no repudiation of what has gone before, no denial of the kind of quotes above. The language may have changed and become less strident, but similar themes of the useful passivity of women remain. Any woman who is not passive (i.e. the feminists) is a "lethal" threat to the family. To be fair, Cardinal Ratzinger does speak of women's valid place in the workforce and in leadership roles in society, and this is certainly to be welcomed. However, the overall thrust of his document is undoubtedly an attack on anyone who argues that women are as capable as men of performing all tasks up to and including the priesthood, which remains reserved, as Ratzinger states, "solely to men".

# Sheltered Workshops
*August 19, 2004*

Joe is in his thirties and has been working at the same job for the past ten years. Like most people, he goes in each day at nine, gets an hour for lunch and finishes at around five. The job isn't great, mainly packing various goods, boring and repetitive. But Joe figures that at least he has work. Most of his friends are not so lucky. Joe gets paid €25 for his 40-hour week. He has no rights, cannot join a union, and can be disciplined or fired at will. He cannot appeal.

Joe is terrified to talk about his work conditions, convinced he will lose his job. Needless to say, Joe is not his real name. You might think that Joe exists in an impoverished third world economy, or perhaps that I am describing work conditions of 100 years ago. But no, Joe lives and works in Dublin today. He is one of the thousands employed in sheltered workshops all over the country. Joe has a disability which means he has difficulty controlling his physical movements. Whether Joe works or not, he gets a social welfare disability allowance, which is about a quarter of the national minimum wage. His actual "wage" of €25 a week is the most his employer says he can afford to pay. There is good news and bad news on the horizon for Joe. The good news is that work has been completed within the Department of Health to develop a code of practice which may give Joe some rights and decent pay. The bad news is that the Department has made no public announcement, so Joe and his fellow workers know nothing about it.

I managed recently to get my hands on a copy of this draft Code of Practice. Its proposals are revolutionary. Those in sheltered employment who are clearly working (as opposed to day-care or therapeutic activity) will be given the legal status and full rights of employees, together with an entitlement to the minimum wage. Estimates vary as to how many people may be affected by this, but out of the 8,000 or so currently in sheltered employment in Ireland, about one third are now in what is considered a standard employee relationship to their employers. It is quite startling to talk to those familiar with this shadowy area of economic activity. "A kind of organised indentured servant structure," was one description of conditions. "Bordering on slavery," was how another expert described the workshops. "Quite a number of multi-national companies exploit this area, getting menial work done on the cheap, and then claim that they're doing their bit for disabled people," he added.

It is important, however, to note here that there are some exceptions to this, where the workshops are well run and the workers are respected and better paid.

However, in the main, thousands of workers with disabilities have for decades been disgracefully treated by a badly-funded system privately run by so-called charitable organisations. People are expected to be grateful that they are being provided with what is euphemistically called organised activity or training, but is often in reality ordinary work. The idea that these workers should enjoy the standard employment rights applicable to the rest of society has simply not been part of the thinking around disability to date.

The new Code of Practice (if it ever sees the light of day) will shake this area to its core. Much space is devoted to the definition of work and of an employee. It separates out day-care and therapeutic activity (which it says should continue to be funded by the Department of Health) from standard employment operations (which should now be transferred for funding and business support to the Department of Enterprise, Trade and Employment). Full rights and pay should be accorded to anyone working in these latter operations, and the Code lists these rights in detail. The Code has been in preparation since 2000, when the ICTU insisted on its inclusion as a provision of that year's national wage agreement, the PPF. A working group was established, and the draft code was delivered to the Department of Health in December 2002. When you ask the Department of Health, as I did, why the secrecy and delay, they'll tell you that it's all really up to the Department of Enterprise, Trade and Employment. This Department, when asked, didn't seem to know much about the area, saying it was a matter either for Health, or for FAS if it involved training. Anyway, they say, they have no money for it in the estimates. Issues also arise with the Department of Social and Family Affairs over whether people with disabilities can work, earn a proper living, and still keep their medical cards and other disability-related benefits. Meanwhile, four years after a commitment to have a proper Code of Practice, Joe still goes to work every day, still earns a pittance, and is still terrified to complain in case he gets fired. Thousands like him are falling between the cracks as government departments try to blame each other for the indefensible delay in ending this exploitation.

# No doubts at stance of Fr Flanagan

*September 9, 2004*

Father Edward Flanagan - or at least his alter ego Spencer Tracy in the Oscar-winning film Boys Town - will be fondly remembered by everyone who grew up in Ireland during the 1960s. That film, together with the likes of The Song of Bernadette, was one of the staples of black-and-white RTÉ, which delighted in movies about heroic Catholics.

Father Flanagan was a renowned children's rights campaigner, and was certainly a hero when it came to bucking the trend of corporal punishment. These days, however, attempts are underway to rewrite the small corner of history occupied by his visit here in 1946. Originally from Ballymoe on the Galway/Roscommon border, Father Flanagan spent all of his adult life in the US, where he founded the famous Boys Town children's home in Nebraska. His philosophy that "there is no such thing as a bad boy" - not even a delinquent Mickey Rooney - underpinned the respect with which that institution treated its young residents. Aeons ahead of his time, he campaigned far and wide against the beating of children, and in 1946 he took that campaign to Ireland. His views condemning the treatment of children in Irish institutions caused considerable controversy. However, Dr Daire Keogh, history lecturer at St Patrick's, Drumcondra, would have us believe that Father Flanagan was interested only in prisons for adults. Writing both in this newspaper last Monday, and in a recent edition of History Ireland, he argues that it is a "mistaken notion" to think that Father Flanagan condemned the treatment of children in industrial schools. Tom Lynch, Boys Town archivist and an expert on the life of Father Flanagan, considers Dr Keogh's view of the priest's concerns to be bizarre. "There are any number of statements from Father Flanagan, both public and private, condemning the way Irish children were treated in the institutions," Mr Lynch told me this week. "It was very well known that he was shocked by what he discovered in Ireland." He talked about the Irish institutions as being like concentration camps for children.

It is difficult to understand Dr Keogh's version of Father Flanagan's views on children's institutions in Ireland. What emerges most powerfully from the priest's statements and writings, both during and after his visit here, is a profound sense of outrage at how children were treated within these institutions. There is not even a hint of ambiguity about this. His own words, written in 1947, best sum up his "main objectives, i.e. - unjust incarceration, unequal distribution of physical punishment both inside and outside the prisons and jails, and the institutionalisation of little children, housed in great big factory-like places, where individuality has been, and is being, snuffed out with no development of the personality of the individual, and where little children become a great army of child slavery in the workshops, making money for the institutions which give to them a little food, a little clothing, very little recreation and a doubtful education." It was this view of the institutions that had prompted Father Flanagan to describe them publicly as "a disgrace to the nation", which received widespread press coverage. Dr Keogh also makes a number of factual errors in his writings about Father Flanagan. His main thesis appears to be that the priest had a high opinion of industrial schools until halfway through his Irish visit, when he was given a copy of the book I Did Penal Servitude by Walter Mahon-Smith. However, a closer reading of Father Flanagan's papers indicates that the priest had read this book before his arrival in Ireland. Consequently, the argument that it provided a turning point simply doesn't hold water.

Dr Keogh is further in error when he states that it was this same Walter Mahon-Smith who provided Father Flanagan with documentation confirming the savage flogging of a child by Christian Brothers at the industrial school in Glin, Co Limerick. This material was in fact sent by local representative Martin McGuire, who at the time demanded a public inquiry into the treatment of children in industrial schools. Dr Keogh refers to Maud Gonne's involvement in the debate on prison reform at the time. However, he neglects to mention her 1946 statement about industrial schools that "the 'Father of Boys Town' warns us that some of these institutions ... need to be changed". Finally, it is worth noting a further quote, this time from Father Flanagan. In private correspondence in 1947, he wrote that "we have no Christian Brotherhood here at Boys Town. We did have them for five years, but they left after they found out that they could not punish the children and kick them around We have punished the Nazis for their sins against society. We have punished the Fascists for the same reason. I wonder what God's judgment will be with reference to those who hold the deposit of faith and who fail in their God-given stewardship of little children?"

# We will pay for carbon emissions
*September 16, 2004*

One group surely delighted with Charlie McCreevy at the moment must be Ireland's SUV drivers. The owners of these monstrous polluters rapidly taking over our city streets have been saved from having to pay more for their gas-guzzling activities by the Minister for Finance's scrapping of the proposed carbon tax. SUVs (sports utility vehicles or big 4X4 jeeps) are one of the more obscene manifestations of new wealth in Ireland. Sales have increased enormously over the past few years (up 35 per cent this year alone), with uncertainty over rising fuel prices providing no deterrent. Most new SUV drivers are not in rural areas, where they might need the extra height and power for off-road driving. The largest growth in sales is in fact to city dwellers, particularly in Dublin, making the SUV the latest, and supremely redundant, status symbol for the middle classes.

Vehicle emissions are identified as one of the major causes of the greenhouses gases currently changing our climate. Carbon-dioxide ($CO_2$) is the most significant of these, and how much is released into the atmosphere depends on the amount of fuel used. With their huge petrol consumption (as high as 24 litres per 100km in some cases), SUVs are increasingly being targeted internationally as an important contributor to global warming. Studies have indicated that they emit up to four times more $CO_2$ than ordinary cars. As a result, several European countries are planning action against SUVs, including banning them from city areas. France and Sweden are leading the way, and there have even been moves in the US, particularly California, to penalise those who insist on pumping such vast amounts of $CO_2$ into the atmosphere. London's mayor, Ken Livingstone, is particularly determined. Calling SUV owners "complete idiots", he said earlier this year that 4x4 vehicles were totally unnecessary and bad for London. In a world becoming more concerned at the effects of climate change, one might imagine that people would now think twice before buying these enormous $CO_2$-spewing vehicles. But not the Dublin middle classes. It seems keeping up with the Jones family is still far more important than the environment. And why not, when you have the Minister for Finance on your side? The most effective way of altering polluting and profligate behaviour is to penalise it. The now defunct carbon tax was to apply across the board, from industry and agriculture to transport and domestic fuel use. Bodies such as the ESRI and the OECD were of the view that a carbon tax in Ireland was necessary in order to alter behaviour throughout society, and so limit the growing damage to our environment. Even the Department of Finance's tax strategy group stated that taxation "represents the least cost and most efficient method of achieving the required reduction in emissions on an economy wide basis, and it is already widely used across the EU and elsewhere in the OECD specifically to target greenhouse gas emissions".

Business interests, however, have been intensively lobbying the Government against such a tax since it was proposed by Charlie McCreevy in his 2002 budget speech. He embarked on a consultation process and received 117 submissions. One of the reasons he gave last week for abolishing the carbon tax was that a majority of these submissions opposed the measure. While this is technically accurate, the exact figure given by himself earlier this year in the Dáil was that 51 per cent were in opposition, hardly an overwhelmingly negative response. Also last week, the Government was peddling the line that the carbon tax would have meant only a tiny reduction in our CO2 emissions of half a million tonnes, about 5 per cent of our total target. However, figures again given in the Dáil by Minister McCreevy (March 2004) do not support this. With the generally accepted tax level of €20 per tonne of CO2, the reduction in emissions would have in fact amounted to more than two millions tonnes, bringing us much closer to our stated commitment to reduce emissions under the Kyoto protocol.

The ESRI has repeatedly pointed out that a carbon tax need not have a negative effect either on households or on competitiveness in industry. It argues that the money raised should be used to offset any hardship caused and also encourage the development of low-pollution alternatives. The experience of Denmark, which has had such a tax for well over a decade with no negative economic impact and a substantial reduction of 9 per cent in greenhouse gas emission, supports the contention that if carefully applied, a carbon tax would ultimately benefit the Irish economy rather than harm it. But that is to take the long-term view. Who knows what government will be in power by the time Ireland has to start paying out multi-billion euro fines for exceeding the CO2 emission levels we have agreed to under Kyoto.

That's likely to be someone else's problem, certainly not Charlie McCreevy's. The motto is live now, guzzle your gas, spew out the fumes, and roll on the SUVs.

# It's time to tell youth about sex
*September 23, 2004*

It was somewhat ironic at the weekend to see former Taoiseach John Bruton extolling Home Rule and deriding the role of the 1916 Rising in gaining Irish independence. Put that against his statement made just over a year ago, that "we spent 200 years fighting for our independence and we get the British Family Planning Association to help us with a sex booklet". Aside from the dubious historical accuracy of this latter view, it does point to double standards to suit the occasion. Mr Bruton was at the time campaigning against a new sex education initiative from the North Eastern Health Board, designed to provide teenagers with unambiguous and non-judgmental information on sexuality. Adapted for Ireland, it was based on tried and trusted measures adopted in the UK. The overwhelming need for such an approach is highlighted by the research published this week from the Crisis Pregnancy Agency (CPA). It shows that younger people have more unprotected sex, more crisis pregnancies, and a higher incidence of abortion than any other age group. Combine that with a "profoundly worrying" lack of knowledge about their fertility and about the morning-after pill, and it is clear that there is a major lacuna in the methods used to provide young people with information about sexuality. In a society where pregnancy has so often become a political and religious football, the value of the CPA-commissioned research is incalculable. For instance, we are at last beginning to see abortion presented in the context of real decisions and choices made by women, as opposed to a purely moral and political issue. Seen from that perspective, the figure of 90 per cent of those under the age of 45 (the sample parameter) now in favour of abortion in some circumstances is evidence that Irish people are finally embarking on the painful process of facing reality. Also interesting were the findings that 95 per cent of women who had had an abortion believed that this was the correct choice for them, and that two-thirds had no regrets.

A second study commissioned by the CPA pinpoints the clear pattern of woefully inadequate sex education. Respondents in this survey (young women between the ages of 19 and 34) spoke of sex education being delivered in schools by teachers either of religion or biology, with an emphasis on the purely biological or on avoiding sex outside of marriage. There was little talk of the kind of choices to be made by young people in engaging in safe sex and using contraception. It is clearly one area where the structure of our education system, delivered in the main under Catholic Church control, is serving to increase the risk of crisis pregnancy among young people. A glaring example of the kind of problems in this area was the fate of the North Eastern Health Board's brave new sex education initiative for young people, the one John Bruton took such exception to. In collaboration with the Irish Family Planning Association, the NEHB was about to launch a number of new booklets designed specifically to appeal to young people between the ages of 12 and 16. 4Boys and 4Girls contained all the information most of us would have killed to have had at that age, presented in a humorous fashion, using uninhibited cartoon illustrations.

But the initiative was killed off before it even started. Various Catholic organisations damned it from a height. Some of the statements were extraordinary - "cheap pornography" and "utter trash", screamed the Catholic Secondary Parents' Association. John Bruton put the boot in. The health board, he said, "should not present a hedonistic view of life". He criticised one of the books for not stating that it is a criminal offence to have sex with someone below the age of consent. Mr Bruton neglected to mention, of course, that the law on age of consent is hopelessly muddled - for girls it is 17, but for boys it is 15. Even more confusing is that a 15-year-old boy can consent to heterosexual sex, but he has to be 17 before he can consent to homosexual sex. Add to this that you can legally marry at 16, and the mind begins to boggle.

You could of course point all this out to young people, but they would likely only end up as befuddled as the rest of us. And the great danger, alluded to by a number of studies, is that if you emphasise the criminality of under-age sex, young people may become afraid to seek either contraception or help in the case of a crisis pregnancy or a sexually transmitted infection. Thanks to the head-in-the-sand brigade, the NEHB's initiative remains shelved. Now, in the light of the CPA research, there is an urgent need to revive it, and to extend it as a national programme, distributing the booklets to schools, youth organisations, parents and, of course, to young people themselves. They in particular have a fundamental right to be informed rather than preached at, to be allowed to protect themselves rather than stumble about in ignorance.

# What does sponsorship really cost?

*October 7, 2004*

Watching RTÉ last Thursday, I was taken aback to see the logo for drug firm Pfizer prominently associated with the station's health programme, The Health Squad. In one of those peculiar coincidences, Pfizer popped up on the News a few moments later, claiming that its arthritis drugs were perfectly safe. The report dealt with the shock withdrawal from the market of Vioxx, an arthritis drug produced by Merck Sharp & Dohme, due to side effects which increased the risk of stroke and heart disease. RTÉ has a long history of allowing commercial sponsorship for some of its programmes. Generally such sponsorship has been unexceptional, with sponsors at one remove from the editorial content of the programme. Aer Lingus sponsoring ER, Kodak for the holiday programme or even Renault for the Late Late Show are sufficiently distanced from content to be unlikely to cause any editorial conflict. However, can the same be said for a drug company sponsoring a health programme? When taken in conjunction with the prominent display of the Pfizer logo all over RTÉ's health website, serious questions now need to be asked about RTÉ's new stated push to increase the numbers of programmes to be sponsored. We are not allowed to know how much Pfizer pays RTÉ for having its logo prominently displayed at the beginning and end of The Health Squad . That is commercially sensitive information, RTÉ says. However, we do know that RTÉ made it available to the market during the summer for a figure of €95,000. RTÉ also points out that the Pfizer sponsorship does not breach its guidelines.

Pfizer is the world's largest drug company. It has nine plants in Ireland and is generally regarded as a good employer. Like many other pharmaceuticals, however, it has been involved in its fair share of controversy. It is connected for instance with the organs scandal, with its subsidiary Pharmacia having received pituitary glands from dead patients through a number of Irish hospitals. It was Pfizer which brought 60 doctors on a trip to France where they attended a Heineken Cup Munster rugby match. This was laudably highlighted by another RTÉ programme (Prime Time , which, according to the station's guidelines, is off-limits for sponsorship). Dr Tom O'Dowd, professor of general practice at TCD, held that for drug companies to take doctors away "on those kind of expensive trips is bribery". Crucially, in the context of the current news about Vioxx, it is Pfizer which stands to gain most, at least in the short term. It makes similar arthritis medication, to which doctors may now turn as an alternative to Vioxx. Leading pharmacological expert Prof Garret FitzGerald has said, however, that questions now need to be asked about the safety of all of these drugs, known as Cox II inhibitors. None of this is to say that Pfizer is any worse or better than most other large pharmaceuticals. It is merely to point out that drug firms have a long track record of being involved in controversies surrounding the medications they produce. In the light of this, it would seem foolhardy to associate a television health programme with a drug company in return for money.

To be fair to The Health Squad, it is not the sort of programme which investigates drug companies or the problems associated with particular medications. What it does do, however, is provide advice to people suffering from a range of common conditions. Were arthritis to be examined, it would certainly be appropriate to deal with patients' worries about medication. The alternative for The Health Squad would be to ignore arthritis, hardly a reasonable option for RTÉ given the widespread and painful nature of the condition. The bottom line here is the risk that the programme's sponsorship will become a factor in the editorial decisions taken about its content. And it is precisely this which the RTÉ sponsorship guidelines, at least in spirit, seek to prevent. RTÉ and other media organisations invariably claim that sponsorship does not affect their editorial decisions, and this may very well be true. But the point is, how can we be sure, when the sponsor may be in a position to benefit directly as a result of the editorial choices made by the progamme makers? In the interests of openness, I must declare an interest here. While working for RTÉ as a producer on Check Up, a health programme broadcast in the 1990s, I argued against proposals to have it commercially sponsored. My opposition was not to sponsorship per se, but rather that I viewed health programming as too sensitive to risk the perception that its editorial integrity might be compromised. Over the years, RTÉ has deservedly earned the confidence of its viewers and listeners in the independence of its editorial content. That relationship of trust with an audience is priceless to any broadcaster, most especially to one which is funded by public money and whose business is public service. It should not be sold for €95,000 or even 10 times that amount.

# Slopping out is rough justice
*October 21, 2004*

Interesting to see the Minister for Justice suing the State (in the shape of Roscommon County Council) over his holiday home in that county. The case relates to the council's refusal to grant an extension of planning permission to Mr McDowell for the construction of his four-storey retreat in Rooskey. It is the second time in just a few weeks that Michael McDowell has been publicly involved in the legal system. "I'll see them in court," he trumpeted in response to the 375 suits being taken against him as Minister for Justice, ironically in respect of another matter to do with building. These cases relate to the absence of toilets in prison cells. Mr McDowell's country residence, we're told, has lots of bathrooms, with all bedrooms discreetly en-suite. In the prisons over which the Minister presides, 800 men are forced to defecate (without privacy) and urinate into pots or buckets, which they must then empty each morning. This is the notorious slopping-out ritual of Mountjoy, Portlaoise, Cork and Limerick prisons.

On foot of a successful legal challenge to the slopping-out regime in Scotland, Irish prisoners are now using the courts system here to highlight similar conditions. Mr McDowell intends to fight them every inch of the way. His Progressive Democrats colleague, Senator John Minihan, has described the prisoners' case as ludicrous, an absolute scam, a blatant attempt to rip off the State. He says their suit should not be tolerated. Despite Mr Minihan's views, the right of access to the courts can no more be taken away from prisoners than it can from the Minister for Justice. It is further enshrined in Irish law that no citizen should be subjected to inhuman or degrading treatment. So the question here in law is whether having to defecate and urinate into a bucket, in the presence of others, and then slopping out the resulting human waste constitutes inhuman or degrading treatment.

The best witness for the prisoners is in fact probably the Minister for Justice himself. "I have no hesitation of saying I found slopping out by prisoners, many of whom are occupying cells on a multiple basis, degrading," he told the Seanad last year. To his own party conference, he used the word "inhumane" to describe the system. Elsewhere he has identified it as both unacceptable and Victorian. The European Commission for the Prevention of Torture (CPT) has repeatedly condemned the slopping out system since 1993. It identified the process as "degrading" and "humiliating", adding that it also debased those prisoner officers who supervised it. In its response, the Irish Government "accepted fully" the CPT condemnation and firmly undertook that all prisons would have in-cell sanitation within seven to eight years.

This of course has not happened, and now the Government and Mr McDowell intend to use taxpayers' money to fight a legal case whose substance they have "accepted fully" for many years. Mr McDowell claims that the Scottish case is significantly different to anything pertaining in this country. However, the slopping-out system in Scottish prisons is in fact almost identical to its Irish equivalent. The judge in question, Lord Bonomy, had no hesitation in finding that it constituted in itself "degrading treatment". In his measured, 85-page judgment, he added that it would induce "shame, disgust, loss of self esteem, low mood, anxiety, tension and anger" in anyone subjected to it. It is not just the Scottish case which stands as a legal precedent supporting the Irish prisoners' claim. Our own courts adjudicated on a similar matter as far back as 1980. A female prisoner in Mountjoy claimed that having to go to the toilet in a bucket and with no privacy violated her constitutional rights. Justice Barrington in the High Court agreed, and only stayed his order to the prison service to rectify matters in the light of a commitment from them that the system was being reformed.

It took almost two decades, but at least now no woman in Mountjoy has to slop out.

Even more disturbing is the fact that the majority of patients in one of our hospitals are also forced to use a bucket for their toilet needs, slopping it out every morning. This too has been condemned repeatedly by almost every inspection body both within and outside the State. The institution concerned is the Central Mental Hospital in Dundrum. That people here are forced to clean their own faeces out of a bucket simply because they suffer from a mental illness is surely the epitome of obscenity. In essence, the State has condemned itself out of its own mouth so often that serious questions now need to be asked about the wisdom of fighting the slopping-out cases in court. It could certainly be argued that the current, aggressive approach, entailing large legal fees and prolonged wrangling, is both wasteful and a reckless use of taxpayers' money. And, as fat fees change hands, a shameful system continues to degrade and humiliate hundreds of men every day of their lives.

# Rip-off Ireland lives on

*November 11, 2004*

The Minister for Tourism, John O'Donoghue, wants us to stop talking about rip-off Ireland in case we scare away the tourists. It's all a myth, he said last week, and the talk of it has gone too far and has to stop. Contrast this with Mary Harney's statement last April that she was "increasingly disturbed by stories of rip-off Ireland and the time has come for some radical new thinking in terms of our approach to consumer issues". Her radical new thinking was to set up an advisory body, the Consumer Strategy Group, to advise on the issue. We haven't heard a peep out of them yet, however. They are not due to report until next year. The reality is that despite Mr O'Donoghue's wishful thinking about myths, rip-off Ireland remains alive and well. Just this summer, we again topped the EU league table as the most expensive member-state for a basket of staple groceries. It is instructive to look at the EU bar chart for this - for most countries, the bars are roughly equally sized, bunched around the average; for Ireland, the bar leaps upwards, showing us a whopping 40 per cent more expensive than most of the rest. When you realise that the rest includes many of the Scandinavian countries, whose high costs we used to speak about with awe 10 years ago, the sheer magnitude of what we have to pay out for ordinary goods on a daily basis is stark by comparison.

We have had the incontrovertible evidence of these somewhat dry, lifeless comparative tables for some years now, but what really brings the contrast to life is people's direct experience of tourism and holidays, both in Ireland and abroad. Stories are legion of Irish people being shocked speechless at how cheap it is to eat out and buy goods literally everywhere else in the world. The same stories are told in reverse by foreigners holidaying here in Ireland. But instead of burying his head in the mythological sand, John O'Donoghue might be more usefully employed in analysing why it is that holidaying in Ireland is so expensive. One element in the explanation is to be found, strangely, in the foot-and-mouth crisis of 2001. Widely presented as a disaster for Irish agriculture, the truth was in fact the direct opposite. A little publicised report published in 2002 by the Department of Agriculture and carried out by independent consultants Indecon laid out the startling fact that the agriculture sector actually benefited financially from foot-and-mouth to the tune of €107 million.

The sector that bore by far the largest economic burden was tourism. The foot-and-mouth outbreak cost it an estimated €210 million for 2001 alone. The Indecon consultants emphasised the likelihood that in fact the cumulative losses would be even greater, with the inevitable knock-on effects into subsequent years.

# Rip-off Ireland lives on

Despite its pleas for help, the Government did very little to alleviate the problems of the tourism industry. This was in sharp contrast to its provision of enormous financial assistance to the agriculture sector. With agriculture accounting for a little over 3 per cent of GDP, compared to 5 per cent for tourism, serious questions need to be asked of the Government's priorities around this issue. The reason of course that agriculture did so well with its somewhat unseemly profits from the foot-and-mouth crisis relates directly to the enormous lobbying power of the farming industry. Put simply, when the Irish Farmers Association shouts jump, the Government meekly asks, how high. When the tourism sector, or indeed the consumer lobby, screams from the rooftops for assistance, it is ignored, or at best thrown the sop of an advisory body to report at some unspecified time in the future. Proper strategic intervention in the aftermath of the foot-and-mouth outbreak could have served to keep prices down in the tourism sector. It is most likely, and hardly surprising, that those involved sought to recoup at least some of their losses by increasing prices. This in turn is now seriously endangering the future of Ireland as an attractive holiday option not just for foreigners, but also for Irish people who are increasingly of the view that you would need to be mad to pay the kind of prices demanded in restaurants, hotels and bed-and- breakfasts around the country. In one of the great understatements of the year, John O'Donoghue says that Ireland has never been a low-cost destination for tourists. It is, he claims, one "for the discerning traveller". The truth, however, is that most travellers with even a modicum of discernment will avoid our high prices like the plague. Sadly, this is not an option open to those of us living here. While up to this point we have alternately fumed and whinged about rip-off Ireland - to very little effect, it should be pointed out - we are now told that we have to shut up about it, in the national interest, of course. This is adding insult to injury. If ever there was a time for the consumers of Ireland to rise up, it is now.

# Bruno's simple request
*November 18, 2004*

Last week saw a flurry of Irish diplomatic activity in the Vatican, where Government secretary general Dermot McCarthy spoke publicly of formalising church/state dialogue, and the Minister for Foreign Affairs, Mr Ahern, met the Pope and invited him again to these shores. As we contemplate the possibility of another papal visit, it is worth considering the extraordinary case of Bruno Hrela. Bruno has a remarkable file of correspondence with the Vatican, from which the following information has been taken.

Bruno was born in Croatia in 1938 into a devout Catholic family. His father was killed during the Second World War when their house was bombed from the air and destroyed. He, his two sisters and his mother, Maria, became refugees and fled to Italy. There they met a fellow Croatian, a priest who suggested to Bruno's mother that she go to Ireland where she could start a new life in that most Catholic of countries.

With this priest's help, Maria Hrela and her family eventually arrived in Dublin in 1951. However, she received little assistance here and was unable to find work. Within months, Maria's children were taken from her and placed in industrial schools. Bruno, then 12 years old, ended up in Artane, which at that time housed up to 800 other boys, and was of course run by the Christian Brothers. As Bruno tells the Pope in his letters, it was here that his personal tragedy began. These letters describe the abuse Bruno suffered as a child at Artane. At the time, he managed to tell his mother what was happening not just to him but to many other boys as well. She was distraught by the accounts of daily beatings and humiliations endured by her son, and embarked on a most unusual course of action. She decided to write to then Pope, Pius XII. Bruno had fluent Italian from his time spent in that country, and so his mother dictated to him and he translated and physically wrote the two-page letter to the Pontiff. It outlined the abuse suffered (physical and sexual, says Bruno) by the boys at Artane, and spoke of the fear and anguish in which they lived. Bruno describes it as a desperate cry for help.

Surprisingly, the Vatican appears to have acted on the letter. Bruno describes a bishop arriving at Artane, with the children all lined up for his inspection. The bishop - Bruno cannot remember his name - was brought over and introduced to Bruno. In front of the Christian Brothers in charge, the bishop asked the boy if he had any complaints about the school. Bruno froze in terror, and did not confirm the accusations of abuse made in the letter to the Pope. The bishop departed, and Bruno was left alone with the Brothers. As he explained in the letters to the current Pope, they beat him into unconsciousness and left him bleeding on the floor. Bruno now wants that original letter, written in the early 1950s, alerting Pope Pius XII to the abuse of children in Artane. He first made the request in 2001. He was curtly informed that the Vatican archives were available for inspection only up until 1922, the end of the pontificate of Pope Benedict XV. Everything since 1922 remains sealed. He has tried again and again, humbly pleading with Pope John Paul, but the response every time is brief and blunt - his request is refused.

All Bruno wants from the Vatican is a copy of what after all is his own letter, written over 50 years ago by his own hand and containing his mother's words. It is, he says, a part of his own story, his own experience. It is almost literally breaking his heart that the Pope won't listen to him. From time to time, Bruno phones me from London, where he has lived for many years. When he talks about Artane and his letter and the current Pope, there often comes a point where he can't continue, where he breaks down and cries. The sadness never leaves you, he says. Of course, were it from the Irish State that Bruno had requested any material relating to himself, he would be given it without argument. His right to any documentation relating to himself is now enshrined in our freedom of information legislation. Perhaps the formalisation of church/state dialogue in this country might be of some value if it avoided abstractions and addressed itself instead to issues such as Bruno Hrela's very simple request from the Vatican. It is one area where the Irish State could teach the Vatican a thing or two about basic duties and obligations, and in the process ease the burden on one man who has suffered much at the hands of both church and state. Twenty-five years ago, when the Pope last visited Ireland, we did not know Bruno's story or those of thousands like him whose lives have been tortured by their experiences as children in Catholic Church-run institutions. Today, in the context of a possible second visit by the Pontiff, we no longer have that excuse.

# Time to come clean on MRSA
*December 2, 2004*

Mary Harney said it all, really. She was flabbergasted at the notes she had been given by her officials in order to answer a Dáil question last October. The question was about MRSA, the antibiotic-resistant infection found in hospitals, and what measures were being taken to control it. Her background notes told her that medical staff were being encouraged to wash their hands. "It seems incredible, but we had to issue guidelines on hand hygiene recently. When I saw this in my briefing note, I had to check whether it was correct," the Minister for Health said. MRSA is a scandal simmering away at the heart of the Irish health service. We have the second-highest rate of infection in Europe, with the figures increasing every year. It is an infection which lives primarily only in hospitals and it targets the sickest of patients. As illnesses go, it is relatively unique in that it is the hospital which gives it to you, and it is hospital which can, if the necessary steps are taken, prevent you from getting it. The primary route of transmission is from the dirty hands, clothing and equipment of medical personnel.

And yet, in Ireland, MRSA is something of a phantom disease. Stories abound of patients and their relatives not being told that MRSA was involved, not knowing why extra precautions were being taken around their cases. There are no figures available for MRSA deaths and each hospital's incidence of the infection remains secret. All we are allowed to have is the overall figure, which tells us that there were 477 MRSA cases in 2003. This is in stark contrast to the UK. They are so alarmed by their MRSA figures that they have introduced league tables comparing each hospital's incidence of the infection. Crucially, they also include MRSA information on death certificates. It is now estimated that the death rate from hospital-acquired infections in the UK may be as high as 5,000, or about one in 10 of hospital deaths. All of this information has put considerable pressure on the British government to act. Without the openness and honesty regarding the scale of the MRSA problem, things would have trundled on much as they were, or indeed much as they still do, in Ireland.

Here, doctors say that it is not fair to compare hospital data on MRSA, as patients may have contracted the infection elsewhere, before a transfer, for example. They also say that it is so difficult to be sure that MRSA was the actual cause of death (as opposed to the underlying illness) that you cannot include it on most death certificates. All of these arguments were made in the UK, but they did not cut much ice. There, a decision was taken that the public had a right to know what their hospitals were doing to them.

Earlier this year British patients were actively encouraged to ask every doctor and nurse if they had washed their hands before touching them. All very well, but such a question could certainly be perceived as offensive, as an implied criticism of the professionalism of medical staff. Hand-washing is so basic a precaution against the spread of infection that one assumes that doctors, of all people, would be aware of it. However, in one of the most damning studies ever undertaken of Irish medics, it was discovered earlier this year that almost half of hospital doctors do not, in fact, wash their hands between patient examinations. Of those who did wash, less than half used disinfectant. Fewer than one in 10 cleaned their stethoscopes once a day (only 2 per cent after each patient). Almost two-thirds wore the same unwashed white coat for longer than a week. There is absolutely no excuse for this degree of outright negligence. Department of Health guidelines on MRSA as far back as 1995 targeted the need for medical personnel to wash hands and equipment between each patient. This was repeated in a 2001 report on a range of antibiotic-resistant infections which stated that these have the potential to reach "catastrophic proportions" within our hospitals. Also ignored have been the repeated calls for additional infection control staff in hospitals, particularly microbiologists. These currently stand at less than half the number considered necessary to control infection. The mid-western region, for instance, still does not employ a single consultant microbiologist, leaving a major hospital such as the Limerick Regional without the necessary protection.

So where, you might ask, are the courts in all of this, why is no one suing? So far, one result of the secrecy around MRSA is that hospitals have remained safe from legal action. If you don't know what you have or what killed your relative, you can't take anyone to court. So, while the costs of the infection are enormous, they are still largely hidden. It is difficult to escape the conclusion that until someone makes the health service pay up in the courts for its negligence in failing to control the spread of MRSA, a significant number of patients will continue to be gravely harmed, or even (secretly) killed, by their stay in hospital.

# Putting the boot into the elderly

*December 16, 2004*

Mary Harney may well wonder what other time-bombs lie in wait for her as Minister for Health. But if she can get away with putting the boot into old-age pensioners, she'll have one up on poor Ernest Blythe, famously crucified for doing just that over 50 years ago. The sheer brazenness of her actions is breath-taking. We overcharged you, but we didn't mean to, so we're not going to pay you back. What we did was unlawful, but we'll rush through legislation saying that it wasn't, and then we'll carry on doing it. Imagine what Ms Harney, that doyenne of probity in high places, would have said if AIB or Permanent TSB had refused to refund the customers they overcharged, or indeed had said that all they could afford was a one-off payment of €2,000 - take it or leave it! That, however, is precisely what she has said to the thousands of pensioners who have been unlawfully overcharged by health boards for their nursing home care. When it comes to Government, it has now been officially confirmed that lower standards apply. For medical card-holders, in-patient care is supposed to be free of charge. A 1976 Supreme Court ruling (in the matter of Maud McInerney) included nursing homes within the definition of in-patient care.

Nonetheless, the Government continued blithely to charge medical card-holders in nursing homes through a variety of means, including the removal of their pensions. The Government now claims that it became aware only recently that this was illegal. However, a look at the annual reports of the Ombudsman shows that the Government was notified at least 16 years ago of the unlawful nature of removing pensions from medical card-holders in full-time care. Since 1988, the Ombudsman has repeatedly ruled that complainants in these circumstances be refunded. This came to a head in the late 1990s, with the special report to the Oireachtas from the Ombudsman on the related issue of nursing home subventions. The Government at that time was forced to refund nursing home patients after it was found that it had not informed people of their statutory right to care, had misled them into believing that this care had to be paid for, had unlawfully included the incomes of people's children as part of a means test to determine the level of fee payable, and had taken 100 per cent of people's pensions from them, leaving them without even the money to buy a newspaper.

All of this had been going on for years, with the full knowledge of the Department of Health that it was illegal. At one stage, the Attorney General's advice was that there was no legal obligation to refund anyone. Sound familiar? The mechanism used by the State to extort the old-age pension from nursing home patients is worthy of Machiavelli himself. On admission to a nursing home, the health boards declare that you have no further need of your medical card, as you are now being fully looked after. So they take it from you. And since you no longer have a medical card, you have lost your entitlement to free care and consequently now have to pay. This sleazy Catch-22 was removed by the 2001 Health Act, which for the first time conferred a medical card as of right on a portion of the population - those over 70.

Incredible as it seems, everyone else has always received a medical card at the discretion of the health boards. Hence their power to remove it at will. The fact that by law they could no longer do so after 2001 for the over-70s left the Department of Health in a quandary. Its decision, based as we're told on an "assumption" of the status quo before 2001, was to keep on removing people's pensions.

Given the Department's public humiliation at the hands of the Ombudsman over such a similar overcharging issue, the ticking of this particular time-bomb must have been deafening. And yet, we are expected to believe that no one in Government heard it.

The current Bill being rushed through the Dáil on the last day of term is likely to have a permanent and disastrous effect on all medical card-holders, not just the over-70s. By redefining in-patient care to exclude that provided in long-stay institutions, it fundamentally alters the hitherto accepted duty of the State to care for those in need.

Such a radical change demands a full public debate. Instead, it will arrive masquerading as an attempt to block a loophole. Mary Harney would be better advised to take her own advice, given earlier this year. Referring to who should pay for care of the elderly, she wrote that "we have to be very cautious about law in this sensitive area". Looking back further, the true enormity of her betrayal of the country's most vulnerable citizens becomes clear. In 1996 she announced that "we want the elderly to be able to live out their retirement in dignity and security without having to worry about the State confiscating their savings".

# Time to reassess Prozac use

*January 6, 2005*

On September 14th, 1989, Joseph Wesbecker walked into his workplace in Louisville, Kentucky, produced an AK47, shot eight people dead, wounded 12 others and finally killed himself. It transpired that Wesbecker had a long history of depression and had been put on Prozac just one month before the killings. Relatives of his victims took a civil case against pharmaceutical giant Eli Lilly, makers of Prozac, arguing the drug was responsible for Wesbecker's murderous rampage. Just last month, documents which should have been produced by Eli Lilly during that case have finally emerged. What they show has sent shockwaves around the world, calling into question the safety of one of the most widely prescribed anti-depressants internationally. Relatives of the Louisville shooting victims had lost their case in 1994. Eli Lilly made full use of its victory, declaring it had been "proven in a court of law… that Prozac is safe and effective". Not only did Eli Lilly withhold damning evidence from the court, however, but it failed to disclose it had in fact already made a secret settlement with victims and relatives during the trial. The judge presiding eventually struck out the verdict that had been so useful to Eli Lilly.

The documents which have now emerged were sent anonymously to the British Medical Journal last month. They include reviews and memos showing possible links between Prozac and suicidal behaviour. They indicate that Eli Lilly was aware of these side effects as far back as the 1980s and sought to suppress the information. The BMJ has now passed on the documents to the US Food and Drug Administration, the all-powerful licenser of medical drugs. It had approved fluoxetine (the pharmacological name for Prozac) in 1987. But Dr Richard Kapit, the FDA clinical reviewer who approved the drug, has said he was not given the Eli Lilly data that has only now emerged. He told the BMJ last month: "If we have good evidence that we were misled and data were withheld then I would change my mind [ about the safety of fluoxetine]. I do agree now that these stimulatory side effects, especially in regards to suicidal ideation and homicidal ideation, are worse than I thought at the time that I reviewed the drug." This is potentially devastating news for anyone on Prozac. While anxiety about its effects and those of a range of similar anti-depressants has been growing in both the US and the UK, there has been relatively little discussion about the safety of these drugs in this country. We are major consumers of anti-depressants, with roughly 1.5 million prescriptions issued in 2003 with about a quarter of a million people in Ireland on anti-depressants. Because of the way in which these figures are presented, it is difficult to be precise on numbers. But we know that roughly 30,000 Irish people took Prozac during 2003, with similar numbers prescribed Seroxat and Efexor. All three of these anti-depressants have been identified as producing worrying side-effects. In addition to concerns about suicide risk, Seroxat has been reported as causing serious dependency. Efexor is recommended to be prescribed only by psychiatrists because of possible toxic effects on the heart. Despite this, it is important to note anti-depressants have been shown to be enormously beneficial to large numbers of those suffering from depression, and have been taken safely by many patients.

Dr Dermot Walsh, former Inspector of Mental Hospitals, has recently raised the issue of over-prescription, however, and the possible links to increased rates of suicide. He notes there is no evidence that these drugs have decreased the incidence of depression. "Worryingly, the rise in suicide mirrors almost exactly the increased use of anti-depressants", he said last month. With our high rate of suicide, there is clearly a need to take Dr Walsh's remarks seriously. Proper, independent research is needed either to prove or disprove any link between the increase in our anti-depressant drug consumption and our incidence of suicide, particularly among the young. What makes this all the more urgent is that it is precisely this group that is most at risk from suicidal and self-harm behaviour when taking some of the anti-depressants. Because of this, the UK and the US recommend that none except Prozac is suitable for those under 18. The European Medicines Agency has recently recommended that not even Prozac should be prescribed for children. Figures for the numbers of Irish children on anti-depressants are not published. Sources indicate, however, that as many as 1,000 children around the country are being given these drugs. Once again, in many cases this is doubtless found to be both beneficial and safe. But in a world where it is clear that some major pharmaceuticals have been less than forthright about the side-effects of their drugs, it is imperative that we in Ireland should begin seriously to question our high rate of prescription of anti-depressants for adults and children.

# Regressing to the bad old days
*January 13, 2005*

In the middle of one night, just before Christmas, there was a knock on the door of the Rathmines refuge for victims of domestic abuse. Lorraine (not her real name) was almost unrecognisable. Bleeding, her face swollen and severely bruised, she had escaped from her home and her violent husband with her five young children. Rathmines, however, was full. They could not take her in. They offered to try to find her an emergency place in a homeless hostel or in a bed-and-breakfast. Lorraine was too frightened for the safety of her children to take up their offer. Faced with nowhere she could feel safe, she returned home and was again severely battered by her husband, leaving her with serious head injuries. This is the reality of life in Ireland for one in every five women who suffer domestic abuse and seek to escape from their violent partners. Women's refuges all over the country are under such pressure that they are frequently forced to turn away women and children whose lives they know may be in danger. In the case of the Rathmines refuge, its manager, Ms Cathy Moore, estimates that they turn away up to 45 families of women and children each month.

This represents a major crisis in the State's provision for victims of domestic violence. The funding for refuges all over the country has been frozen since 2001, representing a significant drop in real terms. It is an area which many people believed had been sorted out since the major battles to have the problem recognised in the 1970s and 1980s. Instead, the reverse has happened, and we are now regressing to the bad old days where an increasing number of women are being denied a safe place of refuge from violent assault in the home. On one level, Imelda (also not her real name) is luckier than Lorraine. Living in the midlands, she has at least had somewhere to go at Christmas for the last four years, since a refuge opened in her town. Each year, her husband arrives home from abroad for the holidays. He rapes her and then he beats her, terrorising their four small children. She has fled the house to her local refuge, which has provided shelter until he leaves again. Imelda has attempted to get barring orders and to have him prosecuted, but, for a variety of reasons, all of this has failed. Her only safety line is the local refuge, which, like elsewhere in the country, is constantly under enormous pressure. So far, she has always been able to get a place, but without additional funding for the refuges, a Christmas may come when she and her children have nowhere to go.

Women's Aid, which runs a national helpline for victims, says that it received 18,902 calls during 2003. Because of lack of resources, it was able to respond to only two-thirds of these, leaving almost 6,000 cries for help unanswered. Figures for last year are currently being compiled, but the situation was, if anything, worse during 2004. The sort of calls received deal with physical, sexual and emotional abuse. Reports range from outright rape in front of the woman's children to scalding and burns, beatings and strangulation, often accompanied by repeated threats to kill both her and her children. In the majority of cases, the aggressor is her husband or partner, and Women's Aid has noted a worrying increase in the incidence of assault against women who are pregnant. A clear sense of the almost epidemic scale of the problem has come from a number of members of the judiciary during the year. Last month, District Justice John Neilan reached the end of his tether. He said that he was appalled by the daily saga of men coming before his court charged with violent assaults on women, many of whom were mothers of their children.

Presiding at Mullingar District Court, Justice Neilan said: "I had it in Longford on Tuesday, and Tullamore yesterday, and again here today. It is running out of control." He stated that he would not tolerate men who "bully, browbeat and assault women" and treat them as pieces of property. Judge Mary Martin has been equally forthright: "I have seen broken bones on women and children, dreadful marks and bruises, physical and mental scars. Domestic violence is very prevalent in this country, and men find it hard to understand that they do not have the right to hit, control, rape, abuse physically, sexually or mentally or manipulate their partners." Given the fact that international research indicates that a woman is likely to have been assaulted 35 times before she goes to the authorities, it is evident that the judges' comments relate to only the tip of the violent iceberg of Irish domestic abuse. In this context, it is shameful that the Government has ignored the issue in each of the last three Budgets. The consequences of such callous neglect have been disastrous for the thousands of women and child victims of domestic violence in this country.

# Nazis, and other animals
*January 20, 2005*

It is revealing to examine what precisely has caused such outrage at the Nazi costume worn by Prince Harry last week. The furore has centred on the crassness of such a choice, particularly coming up to the 60th anniversary of the liberation of Auschwitz, and the offence given to both victims of the Holocaust and Allied combatants.

However, on one level, Harry's choice of costume has an interesting logic to it. The theme of the fancy dress party in question was "Colonials and Natives". To reflect this, the marquee where the party was held was painted white at one end and black at the other. The wearing of Nazi paraphernalia, with its notions of white supremacy and inferiority of non-Aryan races, perfectly complemented the theme of the party. Rather than some mindless display of ignorance, Harry's costume hints at an acute political understanding of the connection between Nazis, colonials and natives. Viewed from this perspective, it could be argued that the prince appears to be something other than the silly boy he has been painted in Britain. British opinion is divided on whether or not Harry should now be allowed into the Sandhurst Military Academy to train as an army officer. The predominant view seems to be that Sandhurst might make a man of him. However, in a piece of remarkably apt timing, it also emerged during the week that a group of Sandhurst cadets has been photographed dressed up as - yes, you guessed it - Nazi officers. Complete with swastikas, one of them can even be seen giving a Hitler salute. In an uncanny echo of the "Colonials and Natives" theme, it appears that those not in Nazi uniform had their faces painted black and wore Afro wigs. Clearly, Harry will fit right in at Sandhurst. Lest anyone think that this colonial business is now just a bit of a joke, the antics of Margaret Thatcher's son Mark should provide a sharp reminder of the views of a certain section of the British ruling class.

Sir Mark was found guilty last week in a South African court of involvement in a plot by mercenaries (some of them ex-British army officers trained at Sandhurst) to topple the government of Equatorial Guinea, Africa's third-largest oil producer. Suspicions have centred on a group of London businessmen keen to get their hands on the country's oil profits. This is the nasty underbelly of what could otherwise be dismissed as the stupid antics of the party-going cream of British society. In the row over Prince Harry and his Nazi gear, the unedifying spectacle of the upper classes disporting themselves at parties celebrating their colonial past has been largely ignored. In the context of past crimes, the activities of British colonists around the world certainly bear comparison with those of the Nazis. However, Britain is far less comfortable dealing with this aspect of its past, finding it easier to focus on the evil of Nazism, and of course by extension on Britain's relatively uncomplicated and honourable record during the second World War. Selective views of the past, and indeed of collaboration with Nazis, have been in evidence recently on this side of the Irish Sea. Sinn Féin Dublin City Councillor Christy Burke announced during the week that he wants Dublin Corporation to pay for the restoration of the Seán Russell statue. Located in Fairview Park, this was vandalised a few weeks ago and its head removed.

Russell had directed an IRA bombing campaign in Britain during the second World War, doing his bit to supplement the damage being done by German bombardment. He had no problem seeking to ally the IRA with the Nazis to fight the old foe. He was considered useful enough by Germany during the war to be ferried back to Ireland in a U-boat, on which he unexpectedly died in 1940.

Leaving aside the raft of complex ambiguities in Ireland towards the Nazi regime during the war, there can be no excuse for such moral compromise today. Regardless of Seán Russell's patriotic activities during 1916 and the War of Independence, the idea that the taxpayer should foot the bill to honour someone who was a Nazi collaborator is an extraordinary proposition. But Sinn Féin would have us remember only a part of Seán Russell's legacy, the easy bit comprising his life before Irish independence. In similar vein, they would also have us forget the shooting of Jean McConville, a widow and mother of 10 children. Referring to party colleague Mitchel McLaughlin's refusal to describe her murder by the IRA in 1972 as a crime, Christy Burke said on RTE's Liveline this week: "We were in an area of conflict let's not go down that route we need to move on." Perhaps a useful way of moving on would be for Dublin City Council to replace the statue of Seán Russell with a memorial to Jean McConville, as a permanent reminder to counter those who persist in their selective and dangerous views of past crimes.

# Baby A demands the truth

*January 27, 2005*

'There are a million questions you want to ask. One door just opens another. And finally you end up with the most basic question of all - why me?" These are the words of the man known as Baby A. He is the only person who so far has had it confirmed to him that he was the subject of an experimental vaccine trial in a mother and baby home in 1960."When I was a baby," he told me when we met some weeks ago, "I was just a number, a category. Why are they still making me feel like that?". The vaccine trials on newborn infants have been the subject of considerable public concern since first exposed over 15 years ago. For a decade, the Government stalled on the issue but finally decided to act.

In a passionate speech to the Seanad in November 2000, the then minister for health Micheál Martin outlined the critical concerns raised by these trials. "The key issue," he said, "that of consent, cannot be fudged because it is fundamental. Children in care have the same rights as other children." He pointed to a number of issues related to the ethical basis of the trials and emphasised that he found the lack of documentation on them both "puzzling" and "unsatisfactory". In 2001 the Oireachtas passed legislation to direct the Commission on Child Abuse to investigate the issue. This was described by the minister as "the ultimate guarantee against a cover-up or whitewash". Referring to those who were the subject of the experimental vaccine trials, he said: "We do not know whether your rights were protected all those years ago, we just do not know, but we believe it is important for you and for the wider society to move heaven and earth to find out." However, the commission's inquiry quickly became bogged down in court challenges. When the Supreme Court ruled in 2003 that Prof Patrick Meenan, who had directed Baby A's 1960 trial, did not have to give evidence, the investigation procedure was shelved. Last summer, it collapsed completely. On application from Prof Irene Hillary, who had conducted a number of the vaccine trials, the court ruled that the Government's order directing the Child Abuse Commission to investigate the vaccine trials was invalid.

When you ask the Department of Health these days how they now intend to pursue the inquiry, what you get is the standard fudge that they are considering the matter - a far cry from "moving heaven and earth" only a few years ago. Baby A - we will call him Peter - finds all of this intensely frustrating. For the sake of his family and small children, he wants to preserve his privacy. But he feels that unless someone speaks out, "the Government will just let this one quietly die away". For most of his life, Peter had no reason to think that there was anything unusual about his background. When his mother died 10 years ago, he began to hear rumours locally that he had in fact been adopted. It transpired that the woman he thought of as his aunt was in reality his true mother. She had been in the Bessboro Mother and Baby Home in Cork, and it was there that four-month-old Peter received the experimental 4 in 1 or Quadrivax vaccine from Prof Hillary in 1960. No evidence has emerged that either he or any of the other babies suffered harm as a result of this. According to Peter, his birth mother (who now lives abroad) has told the Child Abuse Commission that she neither gave nor was asked to give consent to her baby's participation in this vaccine trial, and that she was told nothing about it. Peter also had lived abroad for many years, but found himself so upset by the discovery of his involvement in the vaccine experiment that he has returned to Ireland to find the truth. "It's difficult to explain the effect something like this can have on you," he says. "It has just turned my life upside down. I'm four months old, lying in my cradle, I'm completely vulnerable. I want to know who decided to do this to me and what gave them the right." Peter is one of 58 babies included in the 1960/'61 trial, spread across five mother and baby homes throughout the country. Other vaccine trials to be investigated involved additional children's homes in the early 1970s. Before its investigation was shut down, the Commission on Child Abuse anticipated that evidence could emerge of further trials involving children and babies. In total, they considered that up to 300 infants were part of such trials. As the only one to come forward so far, Peter feels acutely isolated. "The names of the others are there, but no one has bothered to find them. It means I'm the only one fighting to get to the truth here. That makes it even harder when all I feel is that everyone else just wants the whole thing to disappear."

# Health has denied us our rights

*February 3, 2005*

The Department of Health has recently coined an interesting new line in official-speak. "Always under continual review" is the latest phrase, kindly provided to me yesterday when I asked the Department why it had not done what it has been saying for the past seven years it would do. My question concerned Ireland's refusal so far to ratify the Council of Europe's 1997 Convention on Human Rights and Biomedicine. Already signed by 31 European states, the convention now sets the world standard for ethics in medical research and experimentation. Its focus is firmly on rights, underlined by its statement of the primacy of the human being: "The interests and welfare of the human being shall prevail over the sole interest of society or science" (Article 2). Given that much medical research has in the past put the good of society controversially above that of the subjects of such experimentation, this is an important principle to which all civilised countries should subscribe. And yet, Ireland demurs.

The reasons given are spurious. Several ministers for health have explained over the years that the problem concerns provisions in the convention dealing with embryo destruction. But the convention does not deal in any detail with embryo research or destruction. What it does say is that where laws exist to permit such research (and they do not exist in Ireland), then such laws "shall ensure adequate protection of the embryo". And that "the creation of human embryos for research purposes is prohibited". It is difficult to imagine what exactly the Government finds so objectionable in this. A further protocol specifies an outright ban on human cloning, which Ireland has also refused to sign and ratify. We are thus in the extraordinary position of having no legislative control of any kind over human cloning or in-vitro embryo research. But then, of course, we do have the great security of knowing that the Department is keeping the matter "always under continual review". The other mantra trotted out to excuse our laxity in tackling this rapidly developing area of research is that we have to wait for the report of the Commission on Assisted Human Reproduction. The latter was appointed in 2000, and for two years its final report has been promised "within months". We are still waiting.

The fact is that our obsessive concentration on reproductive issues has blinded us to the wider human rights which are the focus of the Council of Europe's biomedicine convention. It deals in detail, for instance, with the issue of consent, especially for those unable to speak for themselves. It specifies children in this context, insisting on proper safeguards. It also states that consideration is to be given to the child's own opinion "as an increasingly determining factor in proportion to his or her age and degree of maturity". Irish law contains no specific protection for children in this regard. We have little excuse for complacency here, given our own examples of the controversial vaccine trials carried out during the 1960s and 1970s on babies in institutional care. At one stage considered a vital and urgent matter for statutory public inquiry, the important concerns raised have now disappeared into the Department's "under review" category. This is particularly worrying as there are several medical professionals who have indicated that as the greater good was served by such trials (i.e. the march towards the elimination of disease), there was nothing wrong with them. The matter of parental consent is seen as being less central in this context. However, it is precisely this balance between the greater good of humankind and that of the individual which the Council of Europe's convention tackles so comprehensively, firmly placing the issue of consent at the heart of any ethical approach to medical experimentation. The convention also deals with issues such as organ retention, an area in which this country has a truly lamentable record. It specifies that fully informed consent must be obtained for any such removal and retention. Further provisions relate to genetic testing and specifically ban discrimination against people on the basis of their genetic make-up. This means, for instance, that insurance companies will not be able to deny cover to anyone with a genetic predisposition to particular diseases. Such discrimination is not yet banned by Irish law.

Overall, the Convention on Human Rights and Biomedicine is perceived throughout Europe as a fundamental statement of protection for all individuals. Some of the 31 countries that have signed up so far have done so with reservations, most of them minor. Each country can exclude any section while still committing itself to the bulk of the provisions. If the Government truly had a serious difficulty with a particular section or article, it could have excluded it. That Ireland has simply ignored the convention in its entirety leaves us as citizens bereft of a significant level of protection now enjoyed by most of our fellow Europeans.

# Not an acceptable target

*February 10, 2005*

There was a time in this country, not so long ago, when a particularly nasty view informed public policy. This was that children born outside marriage were in some way genetically defective. The structures established to deal with these children and their mothers, funded by the State, were premised on the concept that children who were "illegitimate" (in the language of the day) needed to be treated in a particular way to combat the likelihood that they would inherit their mothers' "immoral" genetic make-up. In the context of the attack by Kevin Myers in this newspaper on the children of lone parents as "bastards", and on their parents as "mothers of bastards" and "fathers of bastards", it is worth examining what the consequences of this kind of view meant to tens of thousands of people in this country during the 20th century.

Unmarried women who became pregnant usually ended up in mother and baby homes, most run by nuns. There were two types of these homes: one for what were known as "first-time offenders", i.e. those on their first pregnancies; and others for the "recidivists", those who had given birth before. The effective criminalisation of these women by the use of this kind of language was entirely intentional, and was designed to isolate and stigmatise both them and their children. In terms of the children, the primary target of Kevin Myers' vitriolic abuse, their fate depended largely on whether they were born to "first-time offenders" or to "recidivists". The view was taken that the first category of baby was, subject to a period of careful observation, suitable for adoption. With only a single lapse, their mothers were capable of reformation, and consequently so was the baby. Those women who became pregnant a second time were considered beyond redeeming, with their babies inheriting their mothers' "immorality". Many of these children were transferred to industrial schools, where they made up around one-third of the numbers. This identification of a group of children as being almost part of a genetic underclass goes some way towards explaining the extraordinary levels of abuse and savagery which we now know they suffered at the hands of the religious orders who ran the industrial schools. The use of language, the naming of these children as "bastards" and "illegitimate", played a crucial role in separating them from the rest of society, in defining them as being "other", and in exposing them to rape and battery.

While this experience was common to many children within the industrial school system, regardless of the circumstances of their birth, it was the attitude of overwhelming moral condemnation of single mothers and their children which was so

37

crucial in determining the abusive culture of these institutions. We can take some comfort from the fact that Irish society has now matured to the point where it unequivocally repudiates the attitudes of the past towards lone parents and their children. The recent Crisis Pregnancy Agency public opinion survey showed a resounding 84 per cent of people stating that it is acceptable for a single mother to raise her children alone. Almost two-thirds felt that children of lone parents did just as well as those whose parents were married. The same survey, and all of the recent birth statistics, do not support the contention, put forward by both Kevin Myers and Dr Edward Walsh of the University of Limerick, that teenage pregnancy is rampant in Ireland. What the figures show is that births to teen-age mothers have remained remarkably static in Ireland for the past 30 years, at around 3,000 per annum. What has changed of course is that young mothers now have the option to keep and raise their babies, as opposed to facing the traumas of either adoption or abortion, or even death as in the appalling tragedy of Anne Lovett and her baby in Granard.

We do not in this country have to look to other more extreme examples of the dangers of singling out a vulnerable group of people on the basis of their birth. At a time when the world has again focussed on the horrors of Auschwitz and the Nazi holocaust, we have our own clear lessons from history on the consequences of defining any group of our citizens as being inferior. And this targeting is precisely what happened last Tuesday in this newspaper. As I can attest from personal experience, The Irish Times quite properly adopts a policy of allowing extensive freedom to its columnists to express their opinions. However, in the case of Kevin Myers this week, a line was crossed between the expression of a controversial view (that state benefits encourage lone parenthood) and a dangerous victimisation of a defenceless group of citizens, based only on the circumstances of their birth. It is now important that a statement should issue from this newspaper, not because of its use of terms of vulgar abuse, but in order to repudiate the idea that it is acceptable to target for attack any group of people - children, in this case - who are acutely vulnerable, through no fault of their own, to the consequences of what in effect amounts to an incitement to hatred.

# Piling insult upon injury
*March 3, 2005*

As a display of hypocrisy in action on an extraordinary scale, certain events in Kilkenny over the past three decades are in a league of their own. During the 1970s, the town was the centre of a unique experiment. Led by the local Catholic Church, a progressive scheme was developed to provide State-funded social services to those most in need. It was devised as a possible prototype for the delivery of such services to the entire country, and was at the time universally praised. In the midst of what became probably the most socially conscious part of the country was an institution called St Joseph's. It was run by the same order of nuns spearheading reform across the county - the Irish Sisters of Charity - and catered in the main for the children of the poor. The change in attitude towards poverty sweeping the rest of Kilkenny passed St Joseph's by. Its old, industrial-school culture remained largely untouched. Behind the high walls, where its small inmates were incarcerated, we now know that the nuns employed at least three paedophiles to look after a group of about 30 boys. Several of these children, as young as four, were subjected to over a decade of continuous and savage abuse, both physical and sexual. We know that a number of them told adults of the torture they were suffering. We know that a number of prominent individuals, including the local bishop, Dr Peter Birch, and Sr Stanislaus Kennedy, were made aware of some of the allegations of abuse. We know that for the children concerned little or nothing happened as a result of their complaints.

While there has been a general denial that anyone was told about the sexual abuse, and an insistence that the allegations related only to physical abuse of the children, it is worth recalling the statement given by Sr Stan to the Garda investigation in 1995. Referring to a period during the mid-1970s, she acknowledged that she "picked up on it" that one of the subsequently convicted paedophiles (Myles Byrne) might have been sexually abusing the boys. She added that "with regard to what happened in St Joseph's you simply did not ask". One of those who complained to the nun in charge of St Joseph's at the time, Sr Joseph Conception, was Raymond Noctor. Last Tuesday, he was awarded €370,000 by the High Court in a landmark decision likely to have far-reaching implications for the State. He was only 13 when he told Sr Conception that another of the subsequently convicted paedophiles (David Murray) was "at the boys". It was an act of extraordinary bravery for the child. Murray was a violent and sadistic abuser. He had a large Alsatian dog, of which the nuns were terrified. He would set the dog on the boys, and had taken Raymond out in the dead of night to show him the patch where he would bury him if the child ever revealed what Murray was doing to him. Raymond Noctor's wholly deserved award by the High Court this week is the largest so far received by anyone abused within the industrial schools system. It follows a 2003 case where the courts awarded €75,000 to a man for sexual abuse he suffered in the same institution. The judge described this abuse, a single incident, as being at the lowest end of the scale.

These two cases have now set the range of awards from the courts for institutional child abuse, from €75,000 to €370,000 depending on the seriousness of the abuse and its effects on the victim. What this immediately shows up is that child-abuse survivors are being seriously short-changed by the redress scheme established by the Government to make amends to those whom the State betrayed as children. The average payout from the Residential Institutions Redress Board (RIRB) is only €77,917. The maximum it can pay is €300,000, but just half of one per cent have received over €200,000. The board is mired in conflict with abuse survivors, many of whom have been deeply traumatised by what they perceive as its punitive and hostile approach towards them. The board's operation is also highly secretive, protected by legislation which makes it a criminal offence for the recipient of compensation to reveal any details. However, from similar cases already dealt with, it is possible to estimate that had Raymond Noctor gone to the RIRB rather than to court, he would have received only about a third of the amount awarded to him this week by the High Court. The alarmingly low levels of RIRB awards should be seen in the wider context of the now notorious church/state deal on redress. The Public Accounts Committee report on this deal, due for publication shortly, is expected to be highly critical of the Government. It is an obscene injustice that those abused as children should again be victimised and railroaded by a system desperate to save face (and money), as a result of a bad deal which wantonly exposed the taxpayer and allowed the religious orders directly responsible for the abuse to evade their fair share of responsibility.

# A present from our Charlie
*March 10, 2005*

With the Government flailing about on the nursing homes debacle, Charlie McCreevy must be thanking his lucky stars that he got out when he did. It was, after all, his imperious edict that medical cards be granted as of right to all over-70s that opened up this particular can of worms like a knife through butter. That is not to say it is all sweetness and light in Brussels for Kommissar McCreevy, as he is referred to on the EU website. Coming down the tracks at us is a particularly nasty piece of European law which could wipe away overnight many of the hard-won rights secured by Irish workers. And it is our very own kommissar who has the job of seeing it through. This is the EU services directive, introduced by McCreevy's predecessor at the commission, Dutchman Frits Bolkestein, now a figure of hate across large swathes of Europe, a fate McCreevy must be eyeing with some nervousness.

The directive seeks to enhance competition in service provision across Europe, allowing companies to do business anywhere in the EU without restriction. But of course wage levels and standards of workers' protection vary enormously throughout the EU. Decades of trade union activity in many European countries, including Ireland, have secured wage levels and worker rights far in excess of several of the newer members of the EU, predominantly the eastern Europeans. The services directive confronts this discrepancy head on. If differing rights and benefits structures hinder the free movement of business operations, these rights must simply be dismantled. To level the playing field, it proposes the "country of origin principle". This states that companies will be subject only to the laws of their country of origin, rather than to the standards applying in those countries where they do business.

What this means is that in the case, for example, of a Polish company operating in Ireland, the pay and conditions of its employees need only be in line with legal minimums applicable in Poland. This would apply regardless of the nationality of the workers. The only factor determining their rights would be the location of the company's headquarters.

This immediately opens up the appalling vista of businesses relocating to countries with the lowest wages and worker protection legislation within the EU. Minimum wages could become a thing of the past. Countries might well compete in a race to the bottom to attract companies to locate within their borders. It is conceivable that Irish companies could slash wages and abolish employment rights for Irish workers simply by relocating their headquarters outside Ireland. The potential consequences flowing from the directive, including civil unrest, could be catastrophic.

During the European Parliament hearings on his job as Internal Market Commissioner last October, McCreevy described the services directive as a "visionary" piece of legislation. Arguing that it would facilitate those doing business by removing red tape, he robustly denied that it would have any negative consequences for workers and their rights. The governments of France, Germany, Sweden, Greece, Belgium, Denmark and Portugal strongly disagree. Now mired in controversy, there are indications of divisions in the commission, with McCreevy beginning to distance himself from the directive. The Financial Times has denounced him as craven. He prefers to describe his U-turn as pragmatic.

But what about Ireland in all of this? Debate here as been almost non-existent. To their credit, both SIPTU and Labour MEP Proinsias De Rossa have tried to bring it to public attention and have expressed their strong opposition to the "country of origin principle". The Government has been very quiet. Mary Harney appeared to support the directive last September, saying it was an important step in increasing competitiveness. It has generally been the case that the bulk of EU directives have been of benefit to ordinary Irish people, through providing increased levels of protection across a range of social and environmental areas. The debate over the services directive goes to the heart of what kind of Europe we should have - whether it should seek to protect and enhance the rights of its citizens, or whether it should prioritise the interests of business across the EU.

As part of the "Lisbon Agenda" on economic development, the services directive indicates the most aggressive shift into the pro-business camp which the EU has so far displayed. That any serious debate on this should have passed Ireland by is a poor reflection on a Government which will shortly be expecting us to march, sheep-like, into the polls to pass another piece of EU legislation - its new constitution. With the row over the services directive already threatening to derail French support at the polls for the constitution, we can get some idea of just how concerned the rest of Europe is at the commission's apparent willingness to sacrifice the rights of many of its citizens. It is about time we in this country woke up.

# Refugees need more than law
*March 31, 2005*

Maria and Elizabeth were due to be deported last week on the same plane that removed Leaving Certificate student Olukunle Elukanlo from the country. Both are in their early 20s, and both face the likelihood of one of the most degrading tortures imaginable if they are forcibly returned to their native Nigeria. These are not their real names. Their solicitor has advised them to remain anonymous as they are still going through the legal process, pleading to be allowed remain in Ireland. At the very last minute, he managed to secure a court order to stay their deportation, but it is only a temporary reprieve.

Maria and Elizabeth come from a part of Nigeria where girls and women are routinely mutilated. Their genitals (clitoris and labia) are cut off, often without anaesthetic, and in some cases their vaginas are sown up, leaving only a narrow opening. The reasons put forward locally for this barbaric practice include keeping women pure, enhancing their chances of marriage, reducing their sex drive and risk of promiscuity, and increasing the sexual pleasure of their future husbands. This form of torture is known as female genital mutilation, or FGM. It is common across Nigeria, according to both the UK Home Office and the US State Department. They cite reports estimating up to 60 per cent of Nigerian women have suffered in this way. However, the Irish bodies adjudicating on refugee applications do not appear to take the reality of genital mutilation seriously. Maria and Elizabeth are not alone in being sent back to meet this fate.

Take the experience of Grace Edobor, outlined recently before the Supreme Court. Grace arrived here in July 2002, and was refused asylum. She stated that she had been subjected to FGM in her native Nigeria, and that she feared that her baby daughter would also be mutilated if they were deported. She had been made pregnant by an older man in Nigeria and was being forced to have an abortion by her family. She had refused and fled. A month after she arrived in Ireland, she gave birth to her daughter, who thus became an Irish citizen. However, the prospect of an Irish baby being tortured by having her genitals cut off clearly left the Refugee Applications Commissioner unmoved. Grace was turned down, and lodged an appeal with the Refugee Appeals Tribunal. Despite claims of the vast improvement in speeding up the asylum process, Grace is still, over two years later, waiting for a decision.

The Supreme Court found that the member of the Refugee Appeals Tribunal dealing with her case, barrister Joseph Barnes, had failed in his duty towards her through his "inordinate" delay in reaching a decision. The court upheld the decision by the chairman of the tribunal to reassign her case to another member. Grace will now have to go through the ordeal of a hearing on her harrowing experiences all over again. It transpired in court that Joseph Barnes had built up a significant backlog of cases. Despite this, he was reappointed to the tribunal last January by the Minister for Justice, Michael McDowell. Membership of the tribunal is in the gift of the minister and other members include former Fianna Fáil ministers David Andrews and Michael O'Kennedy, and the former Director of Public Prosecutions, Eamon Barnes. Each is paid per case heard, and their earnings are in addition to their private practice.

The Village magazine has recently highlighted one tribunal member, barrister James Nicholson, as the highest earner at the tribunal, taking in €319,770 during a 28-month period from 2000 to 2003, when his colleagues' earnings averaged €128,000. Nicholson is also identified as rejecting appeals in an overwhelming number of his cases. There have been only "a couple of positive decisions" out of the hundreds he has adjudicated on, according to Frank Brady, head of legal aid at the Refugee Legal Service. We, the public, are not allowed to know the results of the decisions of the members of the tribunal, how many cases each one rejects or accepts. Not even TDs are entitled to this statistical breakdown, as Michael McDowell has stated in the Dáil on a number of occasions.

With such an opaque system, it is not surprising that there are continuous allegations of inconsistency in the decisions handed down by the tribunal. None of their judgments has been published, even though the legislation permits this, with the obvious proviso that confidentiality of applicants be maintained. Last November, the Master of the High Court, Edmund Honohan SC, criticised the basis for many of the appeals tribunal's decisions, pointing out that hundreds of them were being challenged through judicial review in the courts at the expense of the taxpayer.

Michael McDowell has made much of the so-called integrity of the asylum system in recent weeks. He might, however, more usefully contemplate the very real terrors to be faced by young women such as Maria, Elizabeth and Grace, should they be deported by a system in which transparency and accountability appear to count for so little.

# New Pope is no bridge builder

*April 21, 2005*

Five years ago, American nuns were mad as hell and weren't going to take it any more. Their National Coalition wrote an open letter to Pope John Paul II: "In your encyclical, That All May Be One (1995), you asked, 'What changes need to be made in the exercise of papal authority that could make the papal office a source of unity rather than division among Christians?' We would like you to consider silencing Cardinal Ratzinger." The good cardinal had just issued his extraordinary denunciation of all other religious faiths as "gravely deficient". His notorious Dominus Iesus document was produced by the Catholic Church's latter-day Inquisition, better known in polite circles as the Congregation for the Doctrine of the Faith. The nuns, together with a wide swathe of public opinion around the world, were "appalled" by the document. "Cardinal Ratzinger," they told the pope, "sees the goal of dialogue as the conversion of the other party. This attitude creates barriers to dialogue and fosters religious arrogance and bigotry."

Needless to say, the nuns were ignored. In fact, one, Sister Jeannine Gramick, was threatened with dismissal if she revealed that she had been silenced and removed from her ministry by the Vatican for refusing to say if she agreed with another Ratzinger edict - the truly disgraceful one dealing with the "intrinsic moral evil" of homosexual love.

To listen to the reaction in Ireland to the election of Cardinal Ratzinger as Pope Benedict XVI, you'd think he was a cuddly sort of a person, brainy but very, very nice. The unprecedented parade of clerics across the national airwaves fell over themselves to combat his pervasive Panzerkardinal image. But it felt more like a desperate damage limitation exercise than any kind of an honest appraisal of the man's uniquely totalitarian record within the Vatican.

What makes Ratzinger's election so remarkable is that it directly contradicts many of the aspects of his predecessor which had been the focus of such glorification a bare week ago. Key among these was the praise heaped upon John Paul II for his ecumenical work in building bridges between the Catholic Church and other faiths. Ratzinger had in the past voiced criticism of this initiative. In 1986, when Pope John Paul gathered the religious leaders of a number of faiths at Assisi to pray for peace, Ratzinger commented that "this cannot be the model" amid conservatives' fears that such a move would prompt a concept of relativism - that one religion was as good as any other.

# New Pope is no bridge builder

The new Pope's condemnation of relativism was repeated in his homily earlier this week at the pre-conclave Mass in Rome. He conjured up dire images of Christians buffeted around by a long list of "isms". His antipathy to any ideology other than that of "a clear faith based on the creed of the church" has long been a central plank of his belief. It was much in evidence in his successful campaign to suppress those advocating the theology of liberation in Latin America. "Religion must not be turned into the handmaiden of political ideologies," he wrote in his book, Salt of the Earth . But that view has not prevented him from meddling in the recent US presidential election by instructing American bishops that it is wrong to give communion to anyone who favours the availability of abortion; or indeed from stating that Turkey should not be admitted to the EU, being "founded upon Islam" as opposed to Europe's roots in Christianity.

Ratzinger's dismissal of the uproar caused by revelations of clerical child sexual abuse and cover-up as "a planned campaign" was deeply duplicitous - of all the cardinals in Rome, he had a uniquely accurate picture of the enormous scale of the problem, as he had instructed that all reports of clerical abuse were to be sent directly to his office. His profoundly pessimistic and even weird views of women are well known, from his letter to bishops last year attacking feminism as turning women into the "adversaries" of men, to his extraordinary statements about the pill, made in a pastoral letter to his fellow German clerics. "With the pill," he wrote, "a woman's own sort of time and thus her own sort of being has been taken from her. As the technological world would have it, she has been made continually 'utilisable'."

As for the frequently expressed hope by Catholics that the new Pope should have an appeal for young people, it is worth looking at what Benedict XVI has to say about rock music. Addressing the Eighth International Church Music Congress in Rome in 1986, he characteristically did not mince his words. Rock and roll is a "vehicle of anti-religion", he thundered, where man "lowers the barriers of individuality and personality" to "liberate himself from the burden of consciousness". The now official - even, dare we hope, infallible - papal view of rock music describes it as a secular variant of an age-old ecstatic religion, "the complete antithesis of Christian faith in the redemption".

# Farm profit put before our health
*April 28, 2005*

For how much longer will we tolerate the actions of a Government that is threatening our health and making a holy show of us internationally? This week's ruling by the European Court of Justice on Ireland's flagrant breaches of environmental laws on waste disposal is just the latest in a long line of public humiliations that we have brought upon ourselves.

Take for instance the European Commission's efforts to force the Government to ensure we are not poisoned by our own drinking water. It is, of course, extraordinary that such pressure should have to come from outside the State. It is even more remarkable that it has been fought tooth and nail by successive governments over the past 14 years. The nitrates directive has over the years become clouded in all kinds of jargon, and has come to be interpreted as a measure that primarily concerns the agricultural sector. Debate is polarised around derogations from one level of nitrate per kilogram per hectare to another, from nitrate spreading time limits to slurry storage periods. At this point, the eyes of most of us non-farming types glaze over.

In the meantime, our drinking water, our lakes and our rivers continue to be polluted, as the Government thumbs its nose at the EU, the one agency that is trying to save us from our own disinterest. Yet the directive is not the private business of the farming sector - it is a fundamentally important mechanism to ensure the health of every man, woman and child.

Nitrates are one of the nutrients used to fertilise crops and are found in farm waste, principally manure. Every time a farmer spreads slurry on his or her land, nitrates (and other potentially lethal nutrients such as phosphorus) can leach off into ground and surface water. From there they can contaminate drinking water, leading to a variety of severe illnesses, including certain cancers. They also poison rivers, lakes and estuaries by producing toxic algal blooms, where the water takes on a thick, soup-like consistency. This process is called eutrophication - it also has serious implications for both human and animal health.

In Ireland the Environmental Protection Agency is very clear about the problems we face from this kind of pollution. Seventy per cent of our drinking water comes from lakes and rivers, over one-third of which are polluted, according to the EPA. High levels of nitrates have been found in drinking water supplies in 13 counties.

# Farm profit put before our health

Few local authorities are using the powers available to them under the Water Pollution Act to control agricultural activity, which remains the single largest cause of contamination. Although some areas have improved, the EPA emphasises the need for urgent action on pollution of water caused particularly by farm nutrients such as phosphorus and nitrates.

And yet for the past 14 years, successive governments have simply ignored the EU's nitrates directive, whose only purpose is to control the contamination of our water by limiting the amount of slurry that farmers can spread on their land. Not even the most basic initial requirements have been met. In this regard, Ireland stands alone, pariah-like, the only EU country not to have protected its citizens by implementing the directive. Put simply, what has happened is that the Irish Government has placed a higher value on farm profit margins than on public health.

The Irish Farmers' Association has consistently campaigned against the directive, saying that it would put thousands of farmers out of business, using scare tactics to mobilise all farmers to oppose curbs on their slurry-spreading activities. However, the reality is that, according to Teagasc, the vast majority of Irish farmers do not exceed the nitrate limits of 170kg per hectare set by the EU. The small percentage affected are the largest and richest farmers in the country, those who have traditionally dominated the IFA, and those who pollute more and consequently have most to lose from environmental controls. But even for them the Government makes available generous grant schemes for the construction of the necessary additional slurry storage capacity.

It is abundantly clear that moral arguments for the greater good of the population carry little weight with the Government on this issue. Last year's devastating European Court of Justice ruling found against Ireland on every count of breaching the nitrates directive, but has had little impact. The Government blithely continues to argue its entitlement to a derogation that will permit large farmers a much higher maximum level of nitrate application on their land. It is unfortunate from a public health perspective that the EU's patience with such blatant disregard for the law should appear so endless. It has repeatedly threatened to withdraw farm payments and impose daily fines until such time as the directive is fully implemented. It is perhaps only then that the Government may finally be forced to choose between the IFA and the rights of the community to a clean environment, unpolluted lakes, and non-toxic drinking water.

# Drug safety policy hard to swallow
*May 5, 2005*

It is one of the assumptions of daily life that the millions of prescription drugs taken by hundreds of thousands of us each day are safe and have been proven to be so. A body of law, regulation and independent agencies have grown up to protect us in this area and have been able to instil public confidence in the medicines we take. However, major changes are underway in the United States, where the Food and Drug Administration (FDA) has traditionally provided a first line of defence for consumers of medicines all over the world.

An FDA licence for a drug represents the ultimate seal of approval and facilitates its entry into the international market. However, it is happening with increasing frequency lately that major new medications have been running into problems with significantly harmful side effects. Prominent recent examples include several types of anti-depressant drugs, a number of the Cox II-type arthritis drugs, such as Vioxx, and medications, like Baycol, for high cholesterol. Which brings us to the second line of defence for the consumer or, in these cases, the patient. The courts in the US permit the filing of class-action suits, in which large numbers of people harmed in a particular way can bring whoever caused the damage to book.

Class-action suits taken against drug companies have been a critical means of ensuring the safety of medicines, and the accuracy of how they are described and prescribed. While the suits may be taken in the US, regulators around the world - including our own medicines board - sit up and take immediate notice of the outcome of such actions. Even the threat of an action has provided a powerful incentive to force drug companies to withdraw potentially dangerous drugs from the market. Under Irish law, class actions are disallowed, although the Law Reform Commission has argued that there is a strong case for introducing legislation to permit them. So far, no such legislation has materialised, resulting in Irish consumers and patients remaining merely spectators in the large global battles currently taking place mainly in the US between the public and the giant pharmaceuticals.

The Bush administration has moved decisively to curtail the rights of US citizens to take court action against corporations in cases where people have been damaged. This move, somewhat ironically entitled the Class Action Fairness Act, was signed into law by the president last March. It has been welcomed by a delighted coalition of tobacco companies and pharmaceuticals. In addition to this, the FDA has dramatically reversed its drug safety policy, and is now actively siding with drug companies and against consumer interests.

The FDA has begun encouraging pharmaceuticals to use what is known as the pre-emptive defence when they are sued. This allows the companies to argue that since their particular drug has been licensed by the FDA, the responsibility for safety is now that of the regulator rather than the pharmaceutical company's. In this way, drug companies have been getting off the hook, and escaping scot-free as the courts have dismissed a number of recent cases against them.

The architect of this new policy is the FDA's chief counsel, Daniel Troy. He is a lawyer who used to advise the pharmaceutical industry and is a direct appointment of President Bush. He has told drug companies to "make it sound like a Hollywood pitch" when they now seek the willing assistance of the FDA to fight off patients harmed by their medications. This move has been sharply criticised by Margaret Jane Porter, the former FDA chief counsel under Bill Clinton. She has argued that the FDA and the courts system "operate independently, each providing a significant, yet distinct, layer of consumer protection". With the FDA joining the pharmaceutical industry to defend legal cases, one of those critical protection layers for people all over the world is now being stripped away.

Put that together with the recent attempts by FDA management to discredit their own associate director of drug safety, Dr David Graham, when he attempted to draw attention to what he described as the "single greatest drug safety catastrophe in the history of the world" - the licensing by the FDA of the drug Vioxx to treat arthritis. Graham pointed to the fact that the dangers of Vioxx were apparent for several years, during which time up to 139,000 Americans may have suffered heart attacks or strokes directly as a result of taking the drug. He told a US Senate hearing that the FDA is now "incapable of protecting America against another Vioxx". And if America cannot be protected, where does that leave the rest of us? The Irish Medicines Board, and the European network of which it forms part, certainly provide us with an important level of protection. But developments in the US remain a critical factor in determining whether or not a drug is safe. And with the curtailing of class-action suits, which ultimately help to equalise the odds between huge corporations and the ordinary citizen, each and every one of us is the loser.

# Psychiatric profession at it again
*May 26, 2005*

This is the mysterious story of the vanishing Act. Like any other Act, this one started life as a Bill, made its way quite normally through both Dáil and Seanad, and was signed into law by the President. Then it disappeared. Without a trace. No one even went looking for it. And today, few people know it even existed.

This is the extraordinary tale of the Health (Mental Services) Act 1981. It involves the flagrant and deliberate flouting of the democratic will of the people, as expressed through the Oireachtas. It is, in short, a scandal. The 1981 Act provided a range of safeguards and independent appeals for people locked up against their will in psychiatric hospitals. There had been numerous stories of people wrongly committed to psychiatric hospitals, often locked up there for years, with no rights and no way out. Successive governments had promised reform.

You'd be right to think that all of this sounds familiar. We have recently heard much about wrongful committal to psychiatric hospitals, particularly around the case of John Manweiler. Earlier this month he was awarded almost €3 million by the High Court for having been unlawfully detained and wrongly prescribed with medication. Back in 1981, three years before John Manweiler's ordeal at the hands of the psychiatric profession began, the Oireachtas had passed the Health (Mental Services) Act precisely in order to prevent what happened to him and many others like him. That Act had been voted through in the teeth of opposition from psychiatrists, who regarded the establishment of independent tribunals (with non-medical members) to review their diagnoses and committal orders as an unwarranted interference in their professional expertise. This opposition explains much of what became the ultimate fate of a measure designed to protect patients against the abuse of their rights by the psychiatric profession.

All Acts of the Oireachtas contain a provision whereby they must be enacted (or activated) by the relevant government minister. In the case of the 1981 Act, the minister for health at the time, Fianna Fáil's Michael Woods, simply never signed the section to enact it, and nor did any of his successors. So, while it existed as an Act, in reality it never became law. It is, apparently, unique in this regard. Interviewed as part of an RTÉ documentary I made in 1992 on the issue, Adrian Hardiman (then a barrister, now a Supreme Court judge) said: "It is really unusual for this to happen to an entire Act . . . I'm sure it wasn't particularly welcomed by the mental health professionals at the time, but this Act has never been brought into force by the minister and is there on the statute books, a monument to the consensus of parliamentary opinion in 1981, but which other forces have operated to prevent from being brought into law."

Following that 1992 documentary, Fine Gael introduced a Private Members' Bill that contained safeguards for patients similar to those of the neutered 1981 Act. Fianna Fáil, again in government, voted against it and it fell. Despite many further accounts from people locked away in gross breach of their fundamental rights, psychiatric patients continued to be unprotected by law. Throughout all of this, and indeed up to the present, the law governing involuntary committal to psychiatric hospitals has been the Mental Treatment Act of 1945. This confers enormous powers on GPs and psychiatrists to incarcerate people indefinitely, remove their civil rights, and treat them (injection, surgery, ECT) forcibly and without their consent. During the 1990s a handful of people began taking cases on this issue to the European Court of Human Rights. The government was forced to admit that the absence of independent review and safeguards in the psychiatric committal process was a breach of the European Convention on Human Rights.

Which brings us neatly to the Mental Health Act 2001, trumpeted as the solution to all problems around involuntary committal. But, lo and behold, almost four years later, the critical sections of this Act dealing with patient rights and safeguards have not yet been enacted by the Minister for Health, Mary Harney. And the reason? Yes, you guessed it - opposition from the psychiatric profession. Twenty-five years after they successfully stymied the 1981 Act, they're at it again. They are refusing to participate in the three-person tribunal system, designed to review each involuntary committal. Under the 2001 Act, these tribunals cannot function without the involvement of psychiatrists. However, their refusal to co-operate should no longer be allowed to stymie proper protection measures for patients. There are, after all, a number of other mental health specialists who could step into the shoes of psychiatrists perfectly competently on the new mental health tribunals and for the purposes of independent reviews of diagnosis.

The Government now has a simple choice to make. Does it continue, as it has for 25 years, to support at all costs the professional interests of psychiatrists? Or does it choose instead to defend the rights of highly vulnerable people who find themselves in desperate need of protection against those same psychiatrists?

# State fails to protect women
*June 30, 2005*

The court was reportedly stunned by the judge's remarks. It was just over a month ago, and Justice John Neilan was sitting in Longford District Court. The woman before him had asked that her complaint of domestic violence against her husband be withdrawn. Justice Neilan told her that women who back out of complaints in this way "do no service to the female section of the community". He added: "You are only encouraging people to assault you by what you have done here today." It was an honest, if inappropriately harsh, reaction of an officer of the court intensely frustrated by the manner in which many women respond to a system which is supposed to protect them. Justice Neilan had been outspoken in the past on the numbers of domestic violence cases, describing the phenomenon of abuse of women in the home as being "out of control".

What the Amnesty report Justice and Accountability - Stop Violence Against Women published this week makes so clear is that the support systems simply do not exist to assist victims of domestic assault pursue their cases through the courts. And no amount of blaming them when they either do not report an assault or subsequently withdraw a complaint will change that reality. The report indicates that for many women beaten in the home, reporting the crimes perpetrated against them serves only to increase the risks which they, and often their children, may face. With waiting lists of up to three months for barring orders in some areas, it is not surprising that many women believe they may be safer either not to report, or indeed to withdraw a complaint if made.

This represents a major failure for the justice system in this country. That such large numbers of people - overwhelmingly women - are effectively intimidated out of reporting crimes committed against them is a national disgrace. The figures here are stark. Of 8,452 incidents of domestic violence reported to the Garda in 2003 (down by almost 20 per cent since 2002, incidentally), less than half resulted in barring orders from the courts. This should be compared with almost 20,000 calls made to the Women's Aid helpline during the same period, over a quarter of which went unanswered due to that organisation's lack of funding. When we then look at convictions of perpetrators in the courts, figures indicate that successful prosecutions occurred in only 7.7 per cent of these cases. And even within that tiny percentage, Amnesty points to inconsistency of sentencing.

Overall, the vast majority of men who beat, assault and rape their partners get away with it, while most women treated in this way suffer in silence. Amnesty for instance points out that there has not be a single conviction for marital rape in this country, despite specific legislation making it a crime since 1990 and its frequent occurrence as reported by victims to organisations such as Women's Aid. An analysis of the overall figures for rape shows an equally alarming picture. Here there is a vast chasm between the numbers seeking assistance from the rape crisis centres (the Rape Crisis Network Ireland dealt with a staggering 45,000 calls on their helpline in 2004) and the cases ending up in court: a mere 37 in 2004.

The rape crisis centres, which are desperately attempting to provide support to victims effectively abandoned by the State, have been starved of funding for several years. An example of just how low a priority is given to rape can be seen from the lack of forensic facilities for victims around the country. With only five centres equipped to gather physical evidence of rape from a victim, many women (and indeed men and children) have to travel - without washing - for up to four hours to reach a facility where they can be examined. The pattern of lack of State funding is replicated among the voluntary organisations providing sanctuary for the victims of domestic abuse. Amnesty quotes a figure of almost 600 women turned away from refuges, due to lack of space. In many cases, these women had no option but to return, with their children, to the family home - where they were again beaten by their partner.

On the basis of its analysis of the entire area of sexual and domestic violence in Ireland, Amnesty has drawn a conclusion which may have serious implications for the Irish Government as it attempts next month to defend its record on women's rights at the United Nations. Amnesty says international case law is leaning towards the conclusion that physical and sexual violence against women amounts in certain cases to torture and inhuman and degrading treatment under both UN and EU legal definitions. It concludes that the Irish State is itself guilty of these abuses through its failure to act to protect the rights of women affected. Ultimately, it is only by holding the Government to account internationally for its almost criminal neglect of this area that the rights of women will even begin to be realised.

# O'Reilly is the best medicine
*July 14, 2005*

Some years ago, talking to a consultant in one of the major Dublin hospitals, I asked innocently why there was such resistance to allowing people see their medical records. He was genuinely horrified at the thought, saying that doctors would have to completely change how they took their medical notes. In what way, I asked. Slightly sheepishly, he replied that a range of shorthand comments about patients would have to be dropped. Common remarks like STL and TATP "swinging the lead" and "thick as two planks" would just have to be dropped.

It was a rare glimpse into the mentality so evident in the report published recently by Ombudsman Emily O'Reilly on a complaint made by the family of a patient who died in Sligo General Hospital. Her report contains a long list of indignities and inadequacies in care experienced by the elderly man, who died of his illness in 2000 after two days at the hospital. The Ombudsman is highly critical of the treatment received by the patient and his family. Her report is peppered with phrases like "insensitive in the extreme" and "serious failure in communications".

Ms O'Reilly details the interviews conducted by her investigators with all of the key staff involved. She points to inadequacies in medical record keeping, shortcomings in nursing care, and an overwhelming lack of empathy with the family on their bereavement. Staff were unable to tell the man's children whether or not he had received the Last Rites, and they left his effects for collection by them in a black plastic sack under the hospital's Christmas tree.

This was not a case of medical negligence. Nor did it concern lack of resources or funding. It was instead a massive failure of the care system to treat people with dignity, respect or even basic common decency. The Ombudsman's decision to publish in full her report on this case is highly significant. Her willingness to give such exposure to the failures within the hospital system now provides patients with the important option that their complaints will be thoroughly and independently investigated, with recommendations made in public to ensure that the system learns from its mistakes and failures.

There is, however, one problem. The Irish Ombudsman is by law prohibited from examining complaints dealing with the clinical judgements made by hospital doctors.
Unlike her counterparts in Northern Ireland and the UK, she is confined to

examining cases relating only to administrative matters. Furthermore, until recently, many of the large voluntary hospitals were excluded from her remit, all of which probably explains why so few patients and their families have to date taken their grievances to her office. Now, through the publication of the Sligo hospital report, Emily O'Reilly has clearly signalled her intent to become actively involved in this area. "We are very keen to deal with these kinds of complaints," she says, "because who else is going to do it?"

Margaret Murphy is delighted the Ombudsman is so committed to examining patients' complaints. Her son Kevin (21) died tragically after a series of medical errors involving the treatment of his hypercalcaemia (an elevated level of calcium in the blood). The condition is highly treatable, but following a litany of failures at almost every level of the healthcare system, Kevin died in 1999. His family sued a number of doctors and the Mercy Hospital in Cork, and finally won a €76,000 settlement which they gave to charity.

But all Margaret and her family wanted was to hold someone to account for Kevin's death, to ensure the lessons might be learned to prevent such a cascade of failures causing injury or death to anyone else. "I feel the Ombudsman should be able to investigate all matters to do with how patients are treated, including clinical decisions," says Margaret, who has worked since the death of her son for more accountability within the medical system. "If she makes her investigations public and if her recommendations are followed, then it's a much better option for patients and families who have been harmed than either going to court or to the Medical Council."

At present, it is the Medical Council which deals with complaints relating to clinical decisions. As the council is made up principally of doctors, questions have arisen about the ability of the profession to regulate itself in this manner. So much so, in fact, that former minister for health Micheál Martin said last year he intended to bring in legislation allowing patients to appeal Medical Council decisions to the Ombudsman. While this has not yet happened, it clearly signals an acceptance of the principle that the Ombudsman should deal with complaints relating specifically to matters of clinical judgement. But rather than tinkering with a piecemeal system for investigating patients' grievances, it would be of much greater benefit to us all simply to extend the remit of the Ombudsman so she could pursue all complaints relating to all aspects of public medicine.

# Scandal of our mental services
*July 28, 2005*

As sound bites go, it was a good one - Tánaiste and Minister for Health Mary Harney getting her retaliation in first by condemning herself out of her own mouth. Her comparison of parts of the Central Mental Hospital in Dundrum to Nelson Mandela's cell on Robben Island was guaranteed to garner headlines. However, the Minister's timing in issuing this certainly justified criticism of the Dundrum facility was interesting. It immediately preceded the publication of the annual report of the inspector of the Mental Health Services, which contains probably the most damning picture yet of an entire system in crisis.

As a result of Ms Harney's colourful analogy, much attention given to the report centred around the Central Mental Hospital, where conditions are so indefensible there isn't even any point in making the attempt. The Minister, of course, has an answer to that: money has been allocated to eliminate slopping out within months, and anyway, the entire facility is being replaced in the near future, probably on the same site as the new Mountjoy complex.

What the Tánaiste might find considerably more difficult to deal with is the extraordinary picture painted by the inspector of the Mental Health Services of chronic mismanagement and glaring maladministration in the area of psychiatric care, for which, of course, the Minister has ultimate responsibility. Indicating the low priority accorded to mental health, Mary Harney didn't even bother to issue a statement on the inspector's annual report. She showed no such reticence, however, when she announced additional (and much needed) investment in cancer treatment.

Dr Teresa Carey is the new inspector of Mental Health Services, taking over from Dr Dermot Walsh, who for years repeatedly and forcefully criticised the system. What Dr Carey has done in her 550-page report for 2004 is to hone those criticisms into a list of headings, of which the majority - somewhat startlingly - do not relate to the need for additional funding. Of her eight main problem areas, six relate directly to bad management. These are: lack of information management capabilities within the mental health service; lack of clinical governance systems; management deficiencies within the mental health service; lack of accountability for failure to deliver mental health services efficiently; resource mismanagement; and lack of patient involvement in service planning and delivery.

This conclusion is in stark contrast to what we hear from those running our psychiatric hospitals, namely psychiatrists - that the problems all come down to lack of money. While it is certainly true, as the inspector points out, that the entire area has for decades been starved of funds, it is far from the full story. Describing management capabilities as "primitive", Dr Carey outlines the phenomenon of warring factions within different health areas refusing to co-operate with each other. What she identifies as an "unhealthy defensiveness" and "isolationist" operate to neglect fundamentally what is of central importance in any quality mental health service - the needs and priorities of those who use the service.

Ann is one of those who has used the service for almost three decades. She has no doubts about who is to blame for the way she was treated. "It's a draconian system. There's a clear divide between them and us, psychiatrists and patients. It's about power and how they have it all and, in my case, they spent years making me feel worthless and defective," she told me. Ann had been sexually abused by a family member and later as a young woman by a priest. Within a short time, she became profoundly depressed and began what became a pattern of self-harm which lasted for years. "What the system does is degrade you as a person. No one ever bothered to find out anything about my past, or any reason why I was so ill. They labelled me as having a 'retarded personality'. You'd have your odd 15 minutes with the psychiatrist, who wasn't really interested in you, and all you'd get would be more drugs. "If you didn't get better, they wouldn't bother to find out why, they'd just change the drugs...

"It was only when I got out of the system after 28 years and managed to get psychotherapy, that I began to realise that maybe I wasn't such a worthless person after all."

What is described for hospital after hospital in the inspector's report is a model of treatment which is dominated by the psychiatrist, with little or no input from any other specialist. Psychologists, social workers and occupational therapists are clearly regarded as marginal within the system, and multidisciplinary teams function in only a small minority of facilities. While it is certainly true that lack of funding plays a significant role here, it is long past time that we began asking fundamental questions of psychiatrists about their largely unchallenged domination of a system which causes so much misery to so many people trapped within it.

# Everyone has a right to ramble

*August 11, 2005*

After years of beating around the thorny bush of access to private land for those walking the hills of Ireland, farmers have finally come up with a proposal. The Irish Farmers' Association claims that its Country Walkways Management Scheme "addresses the issue of wider access to the countryside". In reality, it does no such thing.

Much of the Irish landscape is dotted with forbidding signs ordering trespassers to keep out, asserting loudly that property is private. Many habitual walkers simply ignore these, but they nonetheless have the effect of creating unease or even fear. When a farmer was jailed last year for threatening a walker on his land, representatives of the main farming organisations met him at the prison gates on his release and publicly supported his stand against trespassers. But Sligo farmer Andy (known as "Bull") McSharry made it clear in newspaper interviews that the issue was really about money. "It's private property," he said at the time. "I'd let them through if they paid."

That is precisely what the IFA's Country Walkways Management Scheme is also about. That each hillwalker would pay each farmer to cross their land is clearly impracticable. The farmers' solution is, as always, to make the State pay, meaning of course the taxpayer. The cost of this scheme, we're told, will be €15 million. Recent activities by the IFA have shown that the issue of access to land is not confined just to hillwalkers. As the ESB proposes to upgrade its pylon network in a number of areas, farmers are seeking substantial compensation for having the poles on their land - up to €18,000 for each pylon, according to one report. Already these demands have delayed one upgrading scheme in Kerry.

There are two distinct and separate issues here. One is people's right of access to the countryside, the other is whether it is fair or appropriate to compensate landowners for work undertaken on pathways, signage and so forth for those walking across their land. On the issue of right of access, the IFA's country walkways proposal is entirely silent. Even if farmers secured payment under it, there is no mechanism to legally force them to remove signs or barriers and to permit access. This absence of legislation to enshrine the right of people to walk the land is at the heart of our difficulties here in Ireland. It is a problem which was equally fraught in the United Kingdom. However, recent legislation there has now firmly established that the principle of the common good is best served by giving the public the right to walk across private farmland.

# Everyone has a right to ramble

The Land Reform (Scotland) Act of 2003, finally introduced earlier this year, is a revolutionary piece of legislation which fundamentally alters the balance between public and private interests over most of the hills, lakes and rivers of Scotland. It gives local authorities far-reaching powers to enforce public access and to remove any attempt to block pathways. All of the arguments we have heard from farmers in this country were employed by Scottish landowners against the reforms. According to Ian McCall of the Scottish Ramblers Association, they tried insisting on getting payment for access to their land and they also argued that they should be fully indemnified by the state in the event of accidents occurring on their property.

However, in Scotland (as indeed here), landowners already enjoy considerable protection against legal action, which was considered adequate by the Scottish legislature. On the issue of payment, Scottish landowners do receive subventions for work carried out on pathways, gates, stiles and signage, but this is in no way tied to the issue of the right of people to cross their land. Crucially in Scotland, this right of access was established before there was discussion of payment for maintenance. In this country, we appear to be approaching the matter backwards, by discussing payment before we have even begun to address the issue of right of access.

In Ireland, such debates invariably end up stymied almost before they begin, by invoking the clincher to all arguments about private property - the Constitution. Landowners have always argued that their constitutional private property rights allow them to determine who is allowed or not allowed on to their land. However, such rights are in fact far from clear and are tempered by the "exigencies of the common good", as the Constitution expresses it. This point was reinforced last year by the report of the Oireachtas All-Party Committee on the Constitution, which stated that "no constitutional amendment is necessary to secure a balance through legislation between the rights of individual owners and the common good". It is therefore a matter for the Dáil and legislation to decide where on this issue the common good lies.

Rather than muddling about, discussing means of giving farmers more money, the Government should establish once and for all the legal right of each Irish person (and indeed visitor) to tramp the hills and vales of this country in peace.

# Fate of the world is in our hands
*August 18, 2005*

It may not be the most popular idea to put forward, but could it be that the current rapid rise in oil prices is actually good for us? The response from many of the sectors involved is predictable. The road hauliers want a rebate in excise duty paid on fuel. They have issued veiled threats that they may blockade ports unless the Government assists them. The Automobile Association, self-styled champion of poor, beleaguered motorists, has called for a reduction in tax on petrol. The Irish Farmers' Association is also looking for a commitment from the Government to reduce tax on farm diesel. What is singularly absent from all the sound and fury about spiralling oil prices is the suggestion that we might respond by reducing our consumption. We know we need to do this anyway in order to slow the rate of global warming, the greatest cause of which is the carbon dioxide emitted by burning fossil fuels. We also know (if we are being honest) that we are in a profound state of denial about the need to fundamentally alter our way of living. If we won't change in the interests of the planet's future, perhaps galloping oil price inflation might make us see sense.

Denial of the appalling reality of climate change is everywhere. In Ireland, it was most evident in the Government's rejection last year of its own plans to introduce a carbon tax. In the US, responsible for one quarter of all the world's carbon emissions, it can be seen in the reluctance to accept that the planet's problems are man-made, and that the solution consequently lies with us alone. That this blindness was orchestrated from within the US administration became apparent earlier this year with the revelation that officials had carefully doctored scientific reports to remove the evidence of the human causes of global warming.

The resulting embarrassment has made George Bush grudgingly accept that human activity does play a part in climate change, but the lack of progress on the issue at the recent G8 summit in Scotland clearly indicates a refusal of the world's largest consumer and most destructive polluter to engage with the need to reduce oil consumption and control carbon emissions. Some hope, however, may lie in the fact that public opinion in the US is changing. A recent Program on International Policy Attitudes poll revealed that 94 per cent of Americans believe that the US should join the international community in cutting carbon emissions. (At present the US has refused to be bound by the Kyoto Protocol, under which most of the world's countries have agreed to reduce their greenhouse gases.)

# Fate of the world is in our hands

While European rhetoric may be more honest about the problem, our actions on this side of the Atlantic remain paltry in the face of what is required. The emissions trading system, whereby an overall limit on carbon emission is set for industry with larger polluters buying unused quotas from cleaner operations, has been criticised for being inadequate. A recent study from the Hadley Centre in the UK has shown that any delay in radically reducing our fuel consumption will only increase the burden on all of us in the long term. Continuing as we are for even the next 20 years will mean that carbon emissions will at that stage have to be reduced up to seven-fold in order to produce the same effect on climate had we acted now.

All of that, of course, is on the level of global politics, making denial of reality that much easier for us as individuals. There is, however, a personal responsibility that each one of us has to the safety of the planet. Are we prepared to give up driving SUVs, significant contributors to global warming, around our cities? And what about cheap air fares, and those frequent flights made to the holiday home abroad now owned by an increasing number of Irish people? Carbon dioxide emissions from aircraft are one of the worst culprits in causing global warming, which makes it almost criminal that aircraft fuel is not subject to tax within the EU, thus allowing fares to remain low even in the face of oil price increases. Just bear in mind that for the shopping day-trip to New York which we're told so many Irish people now like to take, you as an individual will be directly responsible for spewing 2.6 tonnes of carbon dioxide into the atmosphere. Explain that one to the grandchildren when they ask why we did nothing while the planet burned.

There can be few more immoral actions than the conscious act of maintaining our own levels of comfort or even luxury at the expense of the security of not just nebulous generations far into the future, but of our own children and grandchildren. The climate is now changing at such a rate that it is they who will bear the brunt of our selfish abandon. Rather than complaining and looking for handouts, we should embrace the current increase in oil prices as an opportunity to force us to change our destructive and profligate ways.

# Playing to the farming gallery

*September 8, 2005*

You might not have noticed it lately, but it seems we're all living in a police state, one which sets out systematically to criminalise farmers. As the candidates declare themselves in the forthcoming election for IFA president, we can no doubt expect more entertainingly wild statements along these lines. It is all part of the way farmers love to paint themselves as persecuted, and as an election ploy it doubtless plays well to the gallery.

As police states go, mind you, ours is an extraordinarily generous one. According to Teagasc's latest farm survey, farmers last year received, on average, a massive 87 per cent of their income through State and EU direct subsidy. And that's not all. Oh, no. Through a series of measures designed to protect farmers, our police state arranges that consumers (you and I) pay more to them for our food. Figures published by the Department of Agriculture indicate that across Europe, we all pay 26 per cent more for farm produce as a direct result of such protectionist mechanisms. When you accumulate these financial supports for farmers, a paradoxical picture emerges of a sector probably over 100 per cent dependent on State and EU subsidy. In effect, farmers take as much, if not more, from the economy (by way of direct payments and artificially high prices for consumers) as they put into it. We, and the big bad police state, happily cover their losses. We call this the Common Agricultural Policy (Cap).

Even more depressingly, we delude ourselves by denying this reality and spouting platitudes about how important agriculture (and the Cap) is to our economy. The most recent example of this comes from Taoiseach Bertie Ahern. Farmers were delighted by his attack on British Prime Minister Tony Blair last week for daring to criticise the Cap. Blair is "dishonest", said Bertie; the Cap has recently been reformed and we should now leave it alone.

Not good enough, Tony Blair has said, pointing to the fact that the entire subsidy system is flawed and unfair as it disproportionately supports the richer farmers and regions across Europe. His position on this has now been vindicated by one of the largest and most comprehensive studies undertaken of the Cap. Produced by Prof Mark Shucksmith of the University of Newcastle, it analyses who gets what by way of subsidy. Prof Shucksmith shows that the recent, much-vaunted reforms of the Cap have not altered the fact that the rich regions of northern Europe (France, Germany, Britain and the Netherlands) continue to take a much larger share of the pot than the poorer regions of Spain, Italy, and eastern Europe. The pattern of larger and richer farms receiving higher subsidies is mirrored in Ireland. One useful aspect of the Cap reforms, and the move to the single farm payment, is that we can now see clearly for the first time who benefits most from all this largesse. Figures produced over the summer show that top of the list for Ireland was none other than Larry Goodman, whose company Irish Agriculture Development is subsidised to the tune of a whopping half-a-million euro a year or €10,000 a week.

Farm subsidies in general are often presented as simply EU payouts, costing us in this country little or nothing. However, again the reality is otherwise. The Irish Government pays roughly one-third of the total subsidies bill, with its share set to become larger over the next few years. Bertie Ahern's robust rebuttal of any attempts to reform the Cap means that these kinds of handouts, rather than reducing, will remain in place until at least 2013, costing Irish taxpayers more as each year goes by.

There is no joy for any of us either in the views of the Opposition. Enda Kenny surpassed even the Taoiseach by declaring in the Dáil that Tony Blair's attempts to reform the Cap were "simply outrageous". Presumably, Fine Gael also buys into the national myth that agriculture is hugely important to the Irish economy and that reducing farm incomes need all our efforts to support them. A few figures here wouldn't go astray. Farm incomes (again according to the Teagasc farm survey) have increased this year by 5.4 per cent. The great majority of Irish farmers are part-time, with their incomes substantially enhanced by other forms of employment. For those engaged in full-time farming, their incomes increased by almost 8 per cent. All of this quite clearly gives the lie to constant whinging from farmers that their incomes are declining - not to mention the bizarre references to police states and criminalisation. And as for the part played by primary agriculture within the economy? Overall figures put it at just under 3 per cent of GDP. When you factor in the huge direct subsidy, and add to it the indirect support provided by consumers paying artificially higher prices, you reach a figure for the contribution of agriculture to the national economy that is perilously close to zero. Some economists have been pointing this out for years. It seems, however, that no one wants to listen.

# Motoring down road to perdition

*September 22, 2005*

Dublin and Dubliners are in need of a good kick in the behind. The city's refusal to take part in today's European Car-Free Day is just the latest manifestation of its inhabitants' increasing predilection for burying their heads in the tarmac. When taken in conjunction with the results of a recent survey showing that Dubliners are in denial about the reality of climate change, it is becoming clear that the capital is not only out of step with the rest of the country, but is also refusing to take responsibility for the effects of its transport habits.

It is certainly true that the city's efforts on previous car-free days were lampooned as ineffectual and tokenistic. In the last two years, gridlock even seemed to increase on the day in question. That this was the perfectly logical result of closing off certain streets to motor traffic didn't seem to occur to those who condemned the initiative as a failure. But at least in the five years since the start of the Europe-wide designation of the 22nd September each year as a car-free day, Dublin has made some sort of an effort. This year there is nothing. Even the lip-service is gone.

The purpose of the EU car-free initiative was primarily to focus attention on our transport habits and their impact on the environment. It has been an attempt to shift people, if only for one day, towards other, less polluting means of transport. The problem of course in Dublin was that it merely highlighted the inadequacies of the city's public transport infrastructure. It hammered home the reality that the service simply could not cope with any significant number of people leaving their cars at home and trying to get the bus to work. Much of the negativity surrounding the car-free initiative came from those motorists civic-minded enough to use public transport for the day, discovering in the process that either the buses did not go on time, or were full and passed them by. This is the daily reality for thousands of regular public transport users, and the focus on its inadequacies provided by the car-free day was a useful exercise. Equally, it gave cyclists an opportunity to highlight the dangers they experience within the city, and the extent to which cars ignore and intrude into cycle lanes.

However, this year the powers-that-be within the city have decided that since the car-free exercise seemed to cause so much complaint, the solution was to abolish it. And judging from the attitudes of Dubliners to climate change and pollution, it is likely that few will object. Sustainable Energy Ireland this week published the results of a survey designed to analyse public attitudes to global warming and our responsibility for it. Scheduled to mark Energy Awareness Week 2005, it compared the views of people in Dublin, Cork, Limerick, Galway, Waterford and Dundalk. Most startling of the results is that uniquely in Ireland, a majority of Dubliners (57 per cent) do not believe that their actions contribute in any way to climate change. Even president George Bush has stopped trying to get away with that one, which make this level of denial among Dublin's citizens acutely disturbing. Across the rest of the country, over two-thirds of people accept the overwhelming scientific evidence that their actions do indeed have an effect on global warming. Forty-two per cent of Dubliners say that they never think about climate change and that it has no impact on their lives. This compares with 31 per cent nationally and only 15 per cent in Galway, which consistently emerges as the most environmentally aware part of the country. Perhaps the most depressing result was that in Dublin, alone again across the country, a majority of people (55 per cent) said that they were not worried about the impact of the greenhouse effect on future generations. Nationwide, two-thirds of those surveyed said that they were concerned about the effects of global warming into the future, with people in Galway again being the most worried (at 85 per cent).

The polluting habits of Dubliners mirror their lack of concern about climate change and global warming. Sales of sports utility vehicles (SUVs) have increased more rapidly in Dublin than elsewhere. These are not only stupidly unnecessary for urban driving, but are also responsible for a disproportionate share of carbon emissions, the main contributor to global warming. Dubliners also do not share their cars. Recent figures from the Department of Transport indicate that three out of every four cars driving into the city each day contain only one person - the driver. It is against this background that one should perhaps take a somewhat jaundiced view of the recent public whinging about high levels of tax on cars and fuel. The fact that the Government has again dismissed out of hand the arguments for a carbon tax, to curb energy use and emissions, is further evidence of an entire society, and particularly a capital city, happily motoring down the road to perdition.

# Flying the flag of greed

*September 29, 2005*

They are the pariahs of the high seas. They exist in many cases outside the law. The profits of their proprietors take absolute precedence over the conditions of those who work on them. They are the "flags of convenience" ships, where the naked greed of their owners rules supreme.

Irish Ferries is in the process of embracing full membership of this club. Already one of its passenger ferries, the MV Normandy , no longer flies an Irish flag. It was re-registered under the flag of the Bahamas earlier this year. And now, the last remaining Irish-owned passenger ship company is turning its back fully on the Irish flag, making it clear that it intends to re-register all of its ferries elsewhere.

The Bahamas is one of those countries which makes itself available to companies which no longer wish to abide by their own national labour law. The UN Convention on the Law of the Sea states in Article 91 that there must be a "genuine link" between the ownership of a ship and the country where it is registered. There is clearly no link of the kind envisaged in that article between Irish passenger ferries and the Bahamas. Further, the fact that both Ireland and the Bahamas are signatories to this convention has not deterred Irish Ferries in its bid to detach itself from all Irish and EU law designed to protect those who earn their living on Irish ships.

Workers in Irish Ferries have until next Monday to decide whether they will accept either redundancy or a slashing of their pay by up to 50 per cent in some cases and the removal of their legal entitlements to annual leave or even days off, including weekends. Minimum wage, statutory entitlements to leave, working time directives - none of these will apply anymore to Irish Ferries. With the shiny new flags of convenience, be they from the Bahamas or elsewhere, all protection for employees is gone forever.

The Irish Ferries plan is to force out its Irish workers and replace them with cheap labour, probably from eastern Europe. Employing people on 12-hour shifts, seven days a week at around €3.50 an hour is necessary, the company claims, to guarantee continuing profitability. Its tactics have been brutal. It has refused to negotiate or allow any third-party mediation. It has threatened that industrial action will result in a withdrawal of its voluntary redundancy offer of weeks' pay per year of service, leaving workers with either just the bare statutory minimum of two weeks' pay (per year of service), or the wretched salary and conditions on offer if they decide to remain. The company has rejected out of hand the recommendations of the consultants which both it and the unions involved had agreed would analyse options for cutting costs. The consultants' report, finalised last week, suggested among other measures a 5 per cent salary cut for Irish Ferries directors and senior managers.

However, it now transpires that the company had little interest in this exercise. It has been reported that weeks before the consultants produced their report, Irish Ferries was already seeking to recruit cheap foreign labour to replace the Irish staff they are now laying off. You might think from all of this that Irish Ferries was in dire financial straits, about to go to the wall unless drastic action was taken. The reality, however, is otherwise. The company has reported substantial profits for a number of years. While its passenger business has declined on the British routes, this has been more than offset by an increase in its freight operations. And, crucially, its market share in both the passenger and freight areas on the British lines has remained stable.

Irish Ferries has availed of generous tax breaks available in the country whose flag it now casts aside. The introduction of the tonnage tax scheme has saved the company millions in tax. Irish Ferries had threatened to remove its entire operation out of Ireland unless such a scheme was implemented by the Government. In 1991, when the semi-state B&I Line was privatised and sold to Irish Continental Group (ICG, the parent company of Irish Ferries), certain guarantees were given to the government. Séamus Brennan, then minister for transport, told the Dáil that ICG had undertaken to maintain the ships "under the Irish flag". He added that it remained committed to "the maintenance of vital Irish shipping/maritime skills". The privatisation was highly controversial at the time, with Fine Gael accusing the Government of giving away B&I at a rock-bottom price. But at least some of these solemn guarantees allayed fears that such a vital service as our sea connections could be hijacked by unscrupulous private interests.

Irish Ferries has now both flagrantly taken steps which are outside its employee labour agreements, and has made a mockery of commitments given to government. Meanwhile, the country is stripped of its ships and its maritime skills - and our seafarers of their jobs. And despite Bertie's strong words in the Dáil yesterday, so far the same Government has stood by, wringing its hands, "like a bystander at a mugging", in the words of one trade union official.

# Everyone's out of step but Bertie

*October 13, 2005*

It gives me no great pleasure to have to report that our Taoiseach has just recently made a holy show of us in front of the neighbours. It appears to have passed totally unnoticed on this side of the Irish Sea. In the UK, however, it was in full public view.

You may remember the unusually robust attack mounted by Bertie Ahern last month on British prime minister Tony Blair over the latter's criticism of the EU's Common Agricultural Policy (Cap). Delivered by the Taoiseach in a speech at an agriculture fair in Kilkenny, it was followed up by a detailed press release. However, not content with a mere domestic audience for his aggressive defence of the Cap, our leader upped the ante, and on September 26th he penned an article in the rarefied pink pages of the Financial Times, which was an edited version of his Kilkenny speech. The only problem was that some of the crucial figures used by the Taoiseach to support his attack on Tony Blair were wrong. And not just a little bit wrong either. They were wildly inaccurate.

This was pointed out in a letter published in the Financial Times three days later from Stevan Tangermann, director for Food, Agriculture and Fisheries at the OECD, the highly-respected organisation of developed countries of which Ireland is a member.
To bolster his defence of the Cap, Bertie Ahern had produced figures to show that EU subsidy of farmers is not significantly different from similar state support in the US. His thrust was that Cap provisions in Europe are perfectly in line with elsewhere in the developed world. Emphasising the relevance of this comparison, the Taoiseach stated in his article that according to the OECD, "transfers to agriculture from both consumers and taxpayers amount to $103 billion (£58 billion) in the EU and $92 billion in the US, or 1.32 per cent of gross domestic product for the EU and 0.92 per cent for the US." This, he wrote, showed a "broad comparability of support".

However, the OECD never said any such thing. The correct figures actually show the opposite - that EU support of farmers under the Cap substantially exceeds subsidies in the US. Their figures, for the record and as enunciated with devastating clarity in their letter to the Financial Times, are as follows: "transfers to agriculture in the European Union (15 members) were larger than indicated in the [ Taoiseach's] article, namely $132 billion (€117 billion) in 2003, corresponding to 1.26 per cent of GDP." The US figure used by the Taoiseach of $92 billion is, in fact, equivalent to 0.84 per cent of GDP, not 0.92 per cent as he had stated. These figures, however, include all transfers from the state to the agriculture sector, including provision for research and such elements as food stamps in the US. The more important figure when comparing state subsidy of agriculture in the EU and the US is that of direct farmer support. Here the divergence is even more stark: again as pointed out in the OECD letter to the Financial Times, farmers in the EU received in 2003 direct payments of $118 billion (€104 billion) or 36 per cent of farm receipts. In the USA, farmers received only $36 billion or 15 per cent of farm receipts.

It is bad enough that the Taoiseach should have misled the Irish people by using figures which the OECD, with infinite tact, has described as "not exact". That he should then use the same inaccurate statistics to convince the British public of the righteousness of his attack on their prime minister is even worse.

The humiliating rap on the knuckles he has received at the hands of the OECD for getting his sums wrong is entirely appropriate. It should encourage everyone to interrogate his entire premise for supporting measures to subsidise farmers which are becoming increasingly discredited. Of course, it does have to be pointed out that no one in Ireland appears to have noticed the Taoiseach's glaring misuse of figures. But then none of us has the benefit of an enormous staff of personal advisers, no fewer than eight of them in the Taoiseach's department, costing the taxpayer almost €1 million.

With our current concentration on accountability and value for money, it is reasonable to ask how a Taoiseach so powerfully endowed with helpers could have exposed this country internationally to such public embarrassment? I put all of this to the Taoiseach's department yesterday. They told me that the figures used by Bertie Ahern dated from the year 2000, that nothing much has changed, and that they do not accept that they were wrong. So that's alright then. Everyone's out of step but our Bertie. If he decides to use figures that are a full five years out of date, well so what? How dare the OECD or anyone else question him. It of course remains a total mystery as to why he ignored the most recent figures. One wonders just who does he think he is fooling?

# Why it's a good idea to be poor
*October 20, 2005*

Did you know that 75 per cent of Ireland is officially defined as disadvantaged? And further, that this is a great source of pride to the Government? It used to be just over 50 per cent, but hard work and diligence from successive administrations over the past 25 years have brought us up to our current proud level.

I refer to the Disadvantaged Areas Scheme, a mechanism designed to squeeze money out of the EU and give it to farmers. This is part of the Common Agricultural Policy (Cap), which Taoiseach Bertie Ahern and his Government are so desperately keen to defend. And why wouldn't they be? As far as the Disadvantaged Areas Scheme is concerned, it is essentially money for old rope. This is the month of the disadvantaged area payments bonanza, with cheques arriving in the post for over 100,000 farmers in receipt of these compensatory allowances, almost three-quarters of the total number working the land. They don't actually have to produce anything to get the money - it is paid out simply on the basis of how many hectares they own.

Over the past five years, Irish farmers have received well over €1 billion from this scheme alone. On an individual basis, it accounts for about one sixth of their income. Good luck to them, you might say, if the money comes from the EU and doesn't cost us anything, at least directly. However, this is not the case. The Irish Exchequer contributes a substantial amount (over 50 per cent) to this scheme. During the past five years, for instance, the Irish taxpayer has shelled out around €650 million to these vast hordes of poor disadvantaged farmers.

So who exactly is this unfortunate group of individuals? Undoubtedly some of them are indeed working in difficult terrains, in mountainous areas and the like, and do need some form of support. The last time I looked, however, mountainous and inhospitable territory covered nowhere near three-quarters of all the land of Ireland. And further, given that only 70 per cent of our terrain is in agricultural use in the first place, the designation of 75 per cent of the land mass as disadvantaged becomes even more incredible.

The EU itself has expressed concern at the galloping redefinition of land as disadvantaged, or in Euro-speak, "less favoured". In a 2002 report from the European Court of Auditors, Ireland was singled out as being the most extreme example of this.

# Why it's a good idea to be poor

The auditors somewhat dryly remarked that "given that mountainous areas have not changed, the increases [ in less-favoured areas] are all the more remarkable given the advances in soil improvement and varietal development." Their report was a scathing criticism of the EU itself for failing to establish consistent criteria for defining disadvantage, which results in individual countries having considerable latitude in categorising their own land for these additional farmer subsidies.

The Court of Auditors also pointed out that no one had a clue as to whether the scheme was actually doing what it was supposed to. "In the absence of overall evaluation results," its report stated, "no definitive conclusion can be drawn on the effectiveness of the compensatory allowances." With red faces all around, the EU attempted to reform the entire disadvantaged areas scheme earlier this year. Abject failure was the result, with those countries benefiting most from the scheme, particularly France and Ireland, vociferously opposing any change. It is difficult to find any recent Irish evaluation of the Disadvantaged Areas Scheme. It seems to be a case in this country of the less attention drawn to it, the better.

The Mid-term Evaluation of the 2000-2006 Cap Rural Development Programme, carried out for the Department of Agriculture and published in 2003, indicated that in the absence of detailed study, it could not say whether or not the disadvantaged areas payments scheme met its objectives. For instance, the review stated that "it is difficult to conclude whether or not compensatory allowances have contributed to the maintenance of viable rural communities through preventing depopulation". The mid-term review also pointed to the fact that a number of dairy farmers "with relatively high levels of income are now benefiting from the scheme", adding that "this may not be the best targeting of available resources".

Nothing, of course, has happened as a result of this. The scheme remains intact, benefiting farmers large and small, rich and poor alike, all at the expense of the beleaguered Irish taxpayer who persists in the erroneous belief that it is only EU money. This then is a concrete example of the type of agricultural subsidy that Tony Blair in the UK has criticised so trenchantly. All we hear from this side of the water is Bertie Ahern roundly denouncing the British prime minister for seeking reform. That, and a few self-congratulatory pats on the back for having succeeded beyond our wildest dreams in becoming so disadvantaged.

72

# Church role in schools must end
*October 27, 2005*

All the talk is how do we ensure that it never happens again. Given the overall conclusions of the Murphy report on the Diocese of Ferns that two bishops (Herlihy and Comiskey) bad, and one bishop (incumbent Éamonn Walsh) good, is it not now the case that we can all be assured that the Catholic Church has finally put its house in order and our children are safe? Well, no.

One aspect that fairly leaps out of the Murphy report is the question of access, of how it was that so many priests were able to capture such a seemingly endless supply of small victims for their cruel and criminal acts of depravity. This should be a critical question in the minds of each and every parent in this country. The Murphy report makes specific reference to the significant number of paedophile priests who had access to their victims by virtue of their central role of power within schools, at secondary and particularly at primary level.

The State has always run its primary education system along religious denominational lines. While the State pays the entire cost, the schools are actually run by the churches. What this means on the ground is that over 95 per cent of national schools are directly managed by the Catholic Church. In all these cases, the local bishop is the patron of the school, which means that he has effective control through his statutory function to appoint the members of the board of management. These boards are invariably chaired by priests in the area.

For instance, Fr Seán Fortune was chair of the board of management of the primary school at Ballymurn. Canon Martin Clancy used his position as manager of his local school to gain access to and rape girls as young as nine. Fr Jim Grennan's abuse of children took place during school hours as he took them for confirmation classes. Allegations against three other unnamed priests (identified only as Frs Gamma, Zeta and Omega) concern sexual abuse directly related to their activities in local schools.

In Ferns, it was Bishop Herlihy and after him Bishop Comiskey who appointed these priests to positions of such absolute power within the schools. In dioceses all over the country, for which we do not yet (and may never have) the benefit of a report to identify the scale of child rape by clerics, bishops and priests continue to enjoy enormous power over schools and the children within them. It is undoubtedly true that the majority of priests and bishops do not abuse their control over our children. The Murphy report identifies severe failings within the culture of the Catholic Church, however, which it believes ultimately contributed to the abuse of so many children in Wexford. In other words, the failings in Ferns are endemic to the very nature of the institution itself. Chief among these are celibacy and secrecy. It is important to be clear here. The internal rules which the Catholic Church adopts to regulate the behaviour of either its priests or its followers are entirely a matter for itself. However, when it comes to handing over control of virtually our entire education system to an organisation whose very essence has now been unambiguously identified as a risk factor for children, then it is time to reassess in the most fundamental manner the way in which we as a State organise the education of our young people.

We have seen the effects recently of Catholic Church control of major components of our health system, through the scandalous attempts to block clinical drugs trials for cancer patients at the Mater and St Vincent's hospitals. We now have incontrovertible evidence of the incalculable damage done to children resulting in part from Catholic Church control of our schools.

It may be instructive to look at how others have dealt with this problem. The people of Newfoundland in Canada faced during the 1980s and early 1990s an experience very similar to our own present turmoil. They had been deeply traumatised by revelations of widespread abuse of children by priests and Christian Brothers. Like Ireland, Newfoundland had a structure of denominational control of its education and health services. In the space of only a few years, however, it engaged in a series of referendums which radically restructured the provision of these services, transferring them from the power of the various churches into the hands of the state. At what point do we now in Ireland become mature enough as a society to say "enough, no more"? For the safety of our children, it has become imperative that we begin the process of wresting control of our schools from a group of individuals, namely the bishops, who are neither accountable nor answerable to any form of democratic control.

The issues of how our children are educated, who runs our schools and who has access to our children should all be matters for us, the people, to determine through our democratic institutions. They should no longer be subject to the dictates of a celibate, autocratic and secretive caste.

# Reality of church role in schools

*November 3, 2005*

You know you've hit a nerve when you can flush out a prelate on the airwaves. Bishop Leo O'Reilly, chair of the Irish Bishops' Commission for Education, phoned a radio show during the week to protest that really the bishops had very little power within the education system.

My writings here last week produced something in the nature of the standard response of the Catholic Church when its power is challenged - wilful misunderstanding peppered with half-truths. The bishops appear to have collectively decided to take the hit on child abuse. After over a decade of rearguard, damage limitation exercises, full of hair-splitting and Jesuitical economies with the truth, most of them now seem to be in the process of saying "mea culpa". But lay a finger on their prize possession of almost universal control of education in this country, and they come out fighting. Their line that it is the Department of Education rather than the bishops who have the power in this area needs to be critically analysed.

The bishops are patrons of 3,013 or 95 per cent of national schools. On a practical level they exert their power in three main ways. Firstly, they have enormous control over teachers. The local bishop directly appoints the three-member group that interviews and recommends for employment the principals of the schools in his area. He also controls the appointment of all other teachers through his selection of the interview boards for these positions. Since 2002 there is no longer a need for prior sanction from the Minister for Education before the successful candidates are notified. However, prior approval from the bishop remains an absolute requirement. It is important to note that the salaries of these teachers are paid entirely by the State. Secondly, the Department of Education's rules for boards of management of national schools lay out the powers of the bishops. They "may manage the school personally or may nominate a suitable person or body of persons to act as manager". The rules also indicate that the bishop "may at any time resume the direct management of the school or may nominate another manager". In the case where the schools are run by boards of management, the bishops directly appoint the chair of the board and one other member. (Recent figures indicate that local priests chair close to three-quarters of these boards.) Names of other nominees (teacher, parents' and community representatives) must be forwarded to the bishop, and it is he who then formally appoints the entire board. Thirdly, most of the schools are owned by the Catholic Church, despite the heavy investment by the taxpayer in the buildings. Then, of course, there is the notorious "ethos clause" in the 1998 Employment Equality Act, effectively allowing schools to do whatever it takes to protect their ethos.

For the overwhelming majority of Irish teachers, this has profoundly worrying implications for their jobs if they happen to be gay, have sex or become pregnant outside marriage, have an abortion or even use artificial contraception, all of which are deemed contrary to the Catholic ethos. A survey undertaken on behalf of the Department of Education last November showed a strong majority of people in favour of the removal of Catholic Church (and other church) power over education. Almost two-thirds of people (61 per cent) felt schools should be non-denominational. Just over 50 per cent said all religious instruction should take place outside school hours. Only 25 per cent favoured maintaining religious control of schools.

Perhaps in response to this the Catholic bishops went on the offensive a few months later. Last February, Archbishop of Dublin, Dr Diarmuid Martin said schools should have a defined Catholic ethos, verifiable in all its aspects. A few days later Bishop Leo O'Reilly said the time had come to "proactively reassert" the Catholic "agenda" in education. In April Paul Meany, president of the Association of Management of Catholic Secondary Schools, said there was a need for schools to become "really Catholic", adding that young people in them were "a captive audience ... crying out for guidance".

Much of this rhetoric is likely to be fuelled by the fear that shortly there won't be enough priests left to carry out their masters' wishes on school boards. And given the results of the Department of Education survey on religious control of schools, there is no longer a guarantee that the laity will continue to toe the line. On a more fundamental level, however, it is clear that in this area we are being failed by our politicians. Even with the evidence of such a clear majority in favour of the separation of church and State within education, nothing has been done about it. The Labour Party, to be fair, has tentatively suggested that we have State-run national schools. The other political parties remain silent. It is perhaps just one of the practical lessons they could take from the Ferns report, and, at least on this issue, obey the will of the people.

# A torrent of frenzy over Travellers

*November 17, 2005*

Thomas Murphy was living in fear. His brother had been beaten up by a gang of local thugs. A shotgun had been fired into his sitting room. Thomas himself had started carrying a shotgun around with him in case of attack. Last July, he received an eight-year sentence for the manslaughter of Jason Tolan, whom he had shot in the leg with the shotgun, and who had subsequently bled to death. Thomas Murphy pleaded in mitigation that he had acted out of fear. In the 2001 case of William Duffy, the court heard that he was in terror of Paul Rooney, who had arrived at his house demanding methadone. Believing his family to be threatened, Duffy stabbed and killed Rooney. He too was found guilty of manslaughter and also received an eight-year sentence. No public protests followed these cases. There was no evidence of public sympathy for the perpetrators, who were described as "killers" by the tabloid press. Because of the element of fear and the absence of premeditation, the verdicts were for manslaughter rather than murder. But serious crimes had nonetheless been committed and justice had been done.

So why then is it that Mayo farmer Pádraig Nally's six-year sentence for the manslaughter of John Ward has attracted such public outrage? What is it about his case, as opposed to the examples above, that has mobilised people to protest? The one critical difference is that the victim in Mayo was a Traveller, whereas the perpetrator is a settled person. A protest march scheduled for next Sunday in support of Pádraig Nally has been backed by local elements within both the GAA and the IFA, two of the great social forces in rural Ireland. While the GAA head office has distanced itself from the issue, its Mayo secretary, Seán Feeney, has publicly supported the protest against the Nally sentence. In the same interview, he referred to what he described as the occupation of a local playing field by a group of Travellers, encamped there for the past four weeks.

In terms of the IFA, it should be remembered that it also expressed support, in the form of a "freedom rally", for another farmer who took the law into his own hands. This was the case of Sligo man Andy McSharry, jailed last year for threatening a 63-year-old hillwalker trying to cross his land. All this week there has been a torrent of frenzy on the airwaves, much of it focusing on criminality and the Travelling community. Fine Gael MEP Jim Higgins, on RTÉ's Liveline last Tuesday, recited a list of crimes which he said were perpetrated by Travellers over a number of years. The protest on Sunday was to pressurise the Travelling community into getting its act together, he said. There has been no mention of the fact that at the trial of Pádraig Nally, a local Garda sergeant testified that crime in the area, including burglary, was in decline. In 2003, there were five break-ins and 28 reported thefts. The following year, thefts had dropped to a mere 11.

Nonetheless, it is clear that some politicians, principally from Fine Gael, appear to perceive an electoral advantage in stirring up local fears of crime. This on its own is reprehensible and manipulative. However, when combined with the particular social divisions involved in the Pádraig Nally case, it comes dangerously close to an incitement to hatred.

Fine Gael leader Enda Kenny has shown somewhat more restraint by declining to comment on the circumstances of the Nally case. He is confining himself to bringing forth a Private Members' Bill to the Dáil strengthening the legal rights of those who seek to defend their own property against attack.

At present, one is permitted to use reasonable force to protect oneself, although the decision as to what constitutes "reasonable" is ultimately up to the courts. The thrust of the law is to encourage people to avoid confrontation and violence rather than to court it. On balance, there is no evidence that the law in this area is in need of reform, or has served us ill. Given the existence of well over 200,000 licensed firearms, mainly shotguns, around the country, it would seem only sensible that the law should heavily deter anyone tempted to use violence to defend their property.

Mr Justice Paul Carney, the judge who sentenced Pádraig Nally, also presided over the trial of Thomas Murphy, mentioned above. His words during the Murphy case could equally be applied to that of the Mayo farmer: "It is the walking around with a shotgun that has led him to this crime and he has got to take responsibility for that." An inquest jury sitting this week had highly pertinent remarks to make about firearms and their regulation. This was the tragic case of Carlow farmer Michael Kehoe, who shot and killed James Healy over a land dispute, and then committed suicide. The jury's call for urgent reform of the licensing controls for shotguns could not be more timely. It is a recipe for disaster that people driven half crazy by fear of intruders, whether real or imagined, should have such ready access to loaded shotguns.

# What Robinson really said
*December 1, 2005*

Mary Robinson's "copping out" remarks have been given an interesting perspective by the two ESRI studies published this week. Each is revealing in its own different way about the relative positions of men and women in both the home and the workplace.

In the letters columns of this newspaper and elsewhere, Mrs Robinson has been excoriated for something that in fact she did not say. She has been accused of condemning women who opt out of the workforce to care full-time for their children as "copping out". What she actually said was something far more subtle. Her target was complacency. She defined "copping out" not as women leaving paid employment to have children per se, but rather as women "not seeking to have society adjust to let them continue to fulfil their potential". This, she argued, leads us back to the "old problem" of too few women at levels of influence within society. With such power in the hands of men for so long, she pointed out, issues such as gender-based violence and the horrific extent of rape in places such as Darfur, Liberia and Rwanda have not been sufficiently highlighted.

Here in Ireland, we have only to look at the recent figures from Women's Aid that over one-third of women victims of domestic violence are being turned away from refuges because of overcrowding and lack of funding. Mrs Robinson's remarks can usefully be perceived as a wake-up call to women in Ireland, particularly younger women: "A lot is taken for granted - there is a tendency to let things slide and not tackle issues such as violence against women or the hidden barriers that remain to women's progress," she said in the same interview with Róisín Ingle. It is these younger women who are the subject of the ESRI's study, Degrees of Equality - Gender Pay Differentials Among Recent Graduates. Its findings show that young women are as much victims of discrimination as their older counterparts ever were.

Looking at graduates three years into the workforce, the study concludes that women earn on average 11 per cent less than their male counterparts - €590 per week as compared to €660 for men. Women also receive fewer bonuses and fewer training and promotion opportunities than men. For women with undergraduate diplomas, the pay gap widens to 20 per cent. This is in spite of the fact that women generally secure better exam results than men - 74 per cent of women achieved honours grades, compared to 68 per cent of males.

Many of the traditional reasons for women being less well paid than men do not apply to this particular group. Most of the women involved have not yet left the workforce to have children and so have not experienced the drop in pay and opportunity which this often entails. The explanation appears instead to lie in simple, straightforward discrimination. The other ESRI study published this week gives an insight into the respective workloads of men and women in the home. Called the Time Use In Ireland 2005 Survey Report, it shows us that here again, women come off worse. On weekdays, for instance, 71 per cent of men do no cooking or food preparation and 81 per cent do no cleaning. The pattern at weekends is similar.

By contrast, two-thirds of women cook and clean, with the result that they have significantly less leisure time at their disposal than men. With women continuing to shoulder the bulk of the cooking, cleaning and caring for children within the home, as well as holding down a job (for which they get paid less than their male colleagues), one wonders how anyone can view this grim picture with complacency. Part of the reason might lie in the fact that it's not fashionable to be a feminist any more.

Feminism has always meant many things to many people. Lately it has become caricatured as a simplistic and irrelevant ideology which glorifies women's role in the workplace at the expense of those who choose full-time care of their children. However, always at the heart of feminism was the struggle to end discrimination, to provide equal opportunities for women and to redistribute the power within society on a more equitable basis. The current categorisation of feminism as a kind of prescriptive and condemnatory philosophy which says "homemaker bad, working woman good" is an absurd reduction of a campaign which continues to be just as necessary now as it was in the 1960s and the 1970s.

Women today may have more choices, but for many, the options remain unfairly limited. It continues to be vital that women campaign for structures and systems that reflect our (and society's) competing needs for us to fulfil our roles both within the family and in the wider community.

# Dancing night away for charity

*December 8, 2005*

Who are these people who attend charity balls? They must be peculiar creatures indeed, who squeeze themselves with nary a squirm of embarrassment into their obscenely expensive designer gowns and tuxedos, as they parade down the red carpets to do their bit for the less fortunate. What, if anything, goes through their minds as they sip champagne and nibble canapés in aid of the dying, the abused and the maimed, secure in the knowledge that these latter know their place and will never intrude to spoil the fun? The charity balls are usually the major events in the social calendars of the great, the good and the rich of Irish society. They get to dress up, show off their wealth, and rub shoulders with their own kind, all in a good cause, of course. Newspapers and celebrity magazines feed off the events with lavish displays of photographs. A line of text is usually appended giving the amount raised for charity. A warm glow pervades the air at the gorgeous goodness of it all.

In a fashion article in this newspaper a few weeks ago featuring charity ball organisers, one said that her ideal charity event is Elton John's, with its concept of wearing as many diamonds as possible. Another spoke of the downside of €2,000 designer gowns - once you wear them to a ball, it's very hard to wear them again to another event. She assured us, however, that she does get two to three years out of an Armani outfit. A third tells us that she keeps the clothes she likes, but the rest she gives away to one of her "cleaning ladies" (note the plural). These women are a step up on the ladies who lunch, soldiering socially as they do for charity. And it is certainly true that their efforts raise very substantial sums of money for organisations which might otherwise either not survive or have to curtail the services they provide. The charities concerned are rightly grateful for their efforts, as indeed no doubt are the direct beneficiaries of their bounty.

Looking at the area as a whole, though, a few salient features emerge. In general, the charities which benefit from the balls tend to be the less controversial, those which devote themselves to healthcare or medical research, rather than any which seek to effect fundamental change within society. Giving money to a hospital or a hospice through a charity ball does not threaten the status quo. It does not challenge the fairness of a society where some people get to shop for designer gear in New York and Paris while others die homeless on Dublin's streets, outside the glitz and the glamour. Nor does it in any way tackle the fact that hospitals and hospices are in desperate need of this charity as a direct result of the disgraceful underfunding by the State. Such challenges to the way we order this society, entailing as they would the espousal, for instance, of increasing taxes on the wealthy, would most likely be anathema to the charity ball constituency. They are the contents of company boardrooms and their spouses, the shareholders of Ireland, and those much caressed creatures - the entrepreneurs. They are the kind of people who approve, for instance, of the Irish Ferries approach towards maximising profit. They might decry the boot-boy tactics, but you certainly won't find many of them protesting against that company's actions on the streets of Dublin tomorrow. Organising a charity do, to help the victims of the untrammelled pursuit of wealth, would be more their style.

Charity is, and has always been, the easy outlet for the beneficiaries of our inequitable society, who may from time to time feel sorry for the less fortunate. Vehicles for the distribution of largesse were in the past very much the territory of the churches and served to keep the poor in their place by instilling feelings of both gratitude and insecurity. The emphasis was on charity and generosity rather than on the rights of people to services. The charity ball is the shiny, modern, secular replacement, complete with its fringe benefits of networking and securing business contacts. One sales recruitment firm has even singled out the charity ball (together with the golf club) as a most profitable arena in which to do business.

But, like their church-bound predecessors, today's charity fundraisers are also predicated on the principle that the poor and the downtrodden will always be with us.
Nothing about them has the slightest intention of shaking the comfortable notion that there will forever be an unlimited supply of those in need of our generosity, which in turn allows us to surround ourselves with an aura of virtue as we dance the night away.

# Babies born in shame
*January 12, 2006*

The revelations concerning broadcasting legend Frankie Byrne in a television documentary this week point to significant gaps in our understanding of the reality of life in Ireland during the middle decades of the 20th century. Her story adds an important dimension to an aspect of women's lives which has so far attracted relatively little research. The tragic irony of Frankie Byrne's story is the extent to which she, as Ireland's most famous agony aunt, propped up the severe societal norms which had caused her so much pain. The problems which she dealt with on her radio slot from the 1960s to the 1980s were of an innocuous nature, their blandness reinforcing the isolation felt by so many women who had fallen foul of the Taliban-like moral climate of the times, with its uncompromising condemnation of those who, like Frankie, became pregnant outside of marriage.

Frankie Byrne gave birth to a daughter in 1956. Her experience in this regard gives a rare insight into how class distinctions affected the fates of those who became pregnant out of wedlock at that time. While portrayed, undoubtedly accurately, as leading a life of hidden misery as a result of giving up her baby for adoption, Frankie's pregnancy and delivery were considerably easier than for many of her less fortunate contemporaries. With her privileged background and access to funds, she was able to give birth in a private nursing home. Those without money ended up in mother and baby homes, where the regime was often punitive and the moral condemnation absolute.

Even within these institutions, however, money talked. June Gouldring, in her enthralling book, The Light in the Window, has given us a unique account of life here. During the 1950s, she worked as a nurse for nine months in the Bessboro mother and baby home in Cork, run by Sacred Heart nuns. She recounts how women could leave within weeks of giving birth if they paid £100 to the nuns, a substantial sum at the time. Otherwise, they had to spend two years in the institution, working to pay off their keep. Elsewhere, their "sentence" could be up to three years.

Other options for poorer women were to go to one of the Church of Ireland mother and baby homes. These took in women of all religions, and required that they spend only nine months working off their keep. Alternatively, many managed to raise the fare to England, where they could give birth and return home within days. Long before it became a safety valve for Irish women in terms of abortion, the boat to England was the last refuge for those too fearful to give birth in this country. Various Catholic organisations, desperate to safeguard the faith of the infant, patrolled the maternity wards of English hospitals, trawling for Irish women in an attempt to force them to bring their babies home. Many of the infants, however, ended up in a variety of British orphanages, and were eventually adopted. Some remained in institutions from where an as yet unknown number of Irish babies were transported to Australia as part of an extensive child migration scheme which lasted well into the 1960s.

As a general rule, the poorer the unmarried mother, the more gruesome was her fate and that of her child. Babies like Frankie Byrne's, born to better-off women, were more likely to be offered for adoption. Those from the poorer social classes tended to end up in the industrial schools, where they made up roughly one-third of the children within those institutions. It is still only by piecing together the fragments of experiences such as Frankie Byrne's that one can even begin to develop a picture of the complexity of arrangements which existed across the social strata to punish women who broke the arbitrary rules of society.

The most severely affected were those who became trapped within Magdalen laundries, in some cases for most of their lives - a fate reserved for the poorer classes.

Despite a general view that we now know all about the grim nature of life in Ireland during the 1950s and 1960s, we have in fact heard very little about the precise nature of women's experiences within these institutions, or indeed of the detailed structures used by society to confine them. In the midst of the tens of millions quite rightly being spent to compensate victims of children's institutions and to inquire into the abysmal conditions within them, it must surely be possible to find the relatively small amount of money necessary to uncover and record the stories of mothers who also suffered. There remain in Ireland many women and indeed many of their children for whom such a project would serve as a long overdue official recognition of their suffering and a kind of public act of contrition for the persecution that was visited upon them. However, we are already in danger of losing forever their stories, as year by year more of these women take their experiences to the grave. It seems that some secrets may sadly be destined to remain hidden, even in our brand new, shiny Ireland.

# Getting time off to grieve

*January 26, 2006*

The recent emergence of details concerning a Ryanair pilot freezing on a flight from Dusseldorf to Rome raises serious issues. It occurred last September and involved a pilot whose young son had died two days earlier. According to media reports, Ryanair's internal inquiry into the incident refers to the crew's "almost complete loss of situational awareness, both lateral and vertical". The Ryanair report adds that "the first officer repeatedly prompted the captain to ensure he was not suffering some form of partial incapacitation, and when he realised that the aircraft was now in a potentially unsafe situation, he urged the aircraft to perform a go-around, pulled back on the control column and advanced the thrust levers, but he did not assume control from the captain." The aircraft landed safely.

So far, the Ryanair report is the only one to be produced on the incident. As Flight International reported, chief executive Michael O'Leary admitted when the matter became public earlier this month that the airline had "screwed up" by not sending a copy of this final report to either the Irish Aviation Authority or to the Air Accident Investigation Unit. The Italian authorities have also complained that this has delayed their ability to investigate the incident.

All of these various inquiries now under way must of necessity focus on the policy and practice surrounding the consequences of bereavement. This is likely to draw welcome and overdue attention to an issue in the workplace which to date has been largely ignored. Ryanair have said that they do grant compassionate leave to those bereaved, but have changed their policy in response to the September incident on the Rome flight. They have now made it mandatory for all pilots to report a bereavement in the family. Ryanair have said the pilot had not informed them of his loss. We do not yet know why he decided to fly so soon after such a traumatic event. While it is to be hoped that the independent inquiries into the Rome flight incident will extend to examine the issue of these issues, it must be said that awareness of the impact of bereavement and grief on the workplace remains highly limited in Ireland.

Very little research on the area exists for this country, according to the Irish Hospice Foundation, which is now beginning to focus on the issue. The Irish Management Institute do not run any training on it and have never been asked to. The employers' organisations say that they have no specific policy around the issue, but talk of best practice allowing for time off and flexibility. Ibec, for instance, do believe that it is an area worthy of greater attention. "It's fair to say it's a relatively new area," Brendan McGinty, its director of industrial relations and human resources told me, "and the incident in Ryanair certainly raises the profile of the impact of bereavement in the workplace, both in terms of safety and also generally, and that has to be a healthy thing for us all." While there is no legal entitlement in this country to compassionate leave, many companies do provide this, often laying down fixed rules such as three days for a parent, spouse or child, one day for a grandparent or sibling, and so forth.

Many confine their involvement to this, considering it sufficient for dealing with the trauma of their employees.

Roughly 29,000 people die in Ireland each year. The Hospice Foundation estimates that each death affects on average 10 other people, many of whom are currently in employment. It can point to numerous examples of where an overly legalistic approach towards a bereaved employee has soured relations throughout a company. It is convinced that much misery caused by insensitive treatment is silently endured, much as bullying was in the past. Generally, it's a lack of awareness, according to the foundation, which is currently running a series of training seminars on bereavement in the workplace. "Very few organisations are actually bad-minded on the issue," says Breffni McGuinness, the foundation's training officer. "There's a myth out there that if an employer is compassionate, he or she will be taken advantage of, and this hinders a better response from managers. Actually, the opposite is the case. There's American research to show that there's a significant pay-off for companies in terms of staff morale and commitment if they create a culture which is open and flexible and allows people what they need when someone close to them dies." While there are clearly enormous public safety issues involved for companies such as Ryanair in their approach towards employees under stress, the incident on the Rome flight should on a more general level provide an impetus for the treatment in the workplace of those bereaved to become an important matter of public policy and debate.

# Dangers of glorifying the Rising
*February 9, 2006*

Perhaps the most striking aspect of President Mary McAleese's speech on 1916 last month was how old-fashioned it was. Her talk of heroes and sacrifice sounded as if the past 30 years of critical historical analysis of the Easter Rising had never happened. In fact, her rhetoric was rooted firmly within the spirit of 1966.

That year marked the 50th anniversary of the Rising, and it was celebrated with an unholy glee. Military parades abounded. Politicians fell over themselves to be seen reviewing the troops. The Merry Ploughboy was top of the music charts. "I'm off to join the IRA," the nation sang with gusto, "... where the bayonets flash and the rifles crash, to the echo of a Thompson gun." Soldiers lined up on the roof of the GPO, dramatically silhouetted against the sky, pointing their rifles upwards as the four aircraft of the Air Corps flew low along O'Connell Street.

For anyone growing up at the time, it was heady stuff. There could be no greater glory than to die for Ireland. Favoured school children were selected to read the Proclamation to local gatherings all around the country. The really lucky ones got to participate in the enormous pageant at Croke Park. Most dramatic of all was RTÉ's contribution. A bare four years old at the time, the station marked the occasion with its first big drama. Insurrection was broadcast in instalments on each night during Easter Week. It was an all-action series, full of blood, guts and gunfights, with little dialogue to interrupt the excitement. It would be hard to underestimate its impact on the nation. Until then, television drama and movies had always been about other people - cowboys and Indians, Germans and the Allies, cops and robbers on the streets of foreign cities. Now, suddenly, we had our very own goodies and baddies. And in neighbourhoods all over Ireland, we put our toy guns to good use, slaughtering hordes of evil British soldiers in the name of Ireland.

Insurrection was an extraordinary construct when viewed from this distance. A device of reportage was used, with actors playing reporters holding microphones and speaking to camera in the middle of the GPO as bullets and bombs exploded around them. This presentation of drama as incontrovertible fact ruthlessly excluded any other interpretation of events. It was history in black and white - and in more ways than one, as colour had not yet arrived to Irish television. In fact, so visceral was the portrayal of the Rising that I have a clear (but impossible) memory of some of the scenes being in vivid colour, particularly the dying Joe

Lynch, shooting Brits while singing patriotic songs, his face covered in lurid blood. What perhaps best sums up the spirit of the time is a scene from Insurrection in which a group of rebels, surrounded and believing themselves doomed, kneel to say a decade of the rosary in Irish. The camera zooms slowly into one young hero with a pistol in one hand and rosary beads in the other.

The historical adviser to Insurrection was Kevin B. Nowlan, professor of history at UCD. In 1991, on the 75th anniversary of the Rising, he expressed deep unease at the impact of the drama. He felt that it might have led some people to believe "that this kind of activity was good in itself, that it's the right way to proceed in the achievement of a national goal. That kind of effect is one that I would have been, and am still, worried about." There can be little doubt that the smug and wholly uncritical public glorification of violent nationalism in 1966 played a significant part in the emergence of the violence in Northern Ireland three years later. While there are some important differences, the parallels between the 1916 rebels and the IRA of the 1970s and beyond were simply too uncomfortable to allow the Irish State to engage in any large-scale public commemoration of the Rising during the decades of the IRA campaign of violence in the North.

Both groups were unelected minorities whose lack of democratic mandate did not inhibit their claim to act on behalf of the Irish people. The impossibility of celebrating one while repudiating the other was self-evident. Thus there was no significant official marking of the 75th anniversary of the Rising, or indeed of the 80th. Now, as the centenary looms, and with peace in our time, it seems that perhaps it is safe to get back in the water. President McAleese would have us rediscover our heroes, reignite our pride in their selfless sacrifice, and march off again to Dublin, in the green, in the green. But it is not as simple as that. We have learned the hard way that commemorations have a habit of turning into uncritical orgies of celebration with potentially lethal consequences. Perhaps instead of a commemoration, we could more usefully mark significant anniversaries of the Rising with a National Day of Argument, thus ensuring that its messy and complicated legacy would never again become obscured by any sentimental longings for past certainties. To be fair to Mary McAleese, all she was doing was engaging in that argument.

# Justice for Stardust families
*February 16, 2006*

'It's time to move on," was a comment made to one of the Stardust victims by an unknown passer-by at the gathering on the site of the disaster last Tuesday evening. The crass remark was just the latest in a long line of wretched dismissals endured by those whose lives were ripped apart on February 14th, 1981.

It is difficult to avoid the conclusion that the view of that passer-by is shared by official Ireland. It remains to be seen whether the rest of us will care enough to apply the necessary pressure to reopen the Stardust fire and its aftermath to scrutiny. Last Tuesday's event on the Stardust site was not a commemoration. It was an angry protest. The business of "moving on" had been taken very seriously indeed by the owners of the Stardust, Patrick Butterly & Sons Ltd.

It emerged that of all nights, the precise 25th anniversary of the inferno was chosen as the date for the opening of a newly-refurbished pub at the location, with a drinks licence in the name Patrick Butterly & Sons Ltd. As we have been usefully reminded during the week, the tribunal of inquiry into the Stardust fire found that the owner Eamon Butterly had acted with "reckless disregard" for the safety of those on the premises. The locked fire exits, the breaching of fire regulations, the failure to comply with public safety bylaws were all clearly catalogued by that tribunal. The State was also held to be negligent. Insufficient action had been taken when it was discovered that regulations were being flouted, particularly those relating to fire exits.

There were serious errors and omissions in the conversion of the building, together with breaches of requirements of the chief fire officer, relevant bylaws and the fire protection standards of the Department of the Environment. All of this contributed to 48 deaths, according to the inquiry. And yet, no one was held to account. The finding of the tribunal that arson was the probable cause of the fire, despite any clear evidence to support this, diverted the emphasis away from the combined negligence of the State and the Stardust owners. It shifted the primary responsibility for the tragedy on to person or persons unknown, thus diffusing the relatives' and survivors' demands for justice.

The courts were never asked to rule on civil liability for the disaster. Hundreds of victims tried to take legal action, but the obstacles were enormous. The prohibition on class actions, long delays within the system, and mounting legal costs all conspired to make them choose instead the route of the compensation tribunal set up in 1985. While established in good faith to assist the victims, this particular tribunal served to protect both the State and the Stardust owners from any direct court finding to determine the extent of their liability for the disaster. In choosing compensation, the victims had to agree not to pursue any further legal action in respect of their injuries or loss. They were left with little choice, and many felt that they were being paid off to shut them up and quietly close the chapter on the Stardust. It was shocking to have it pointed out again that the loss of a child was pegged at a mere £7,500, and that in the case of the Keegan family who lost two daughters, their father John was turned down even for that.

Even when the Stardust victims attempted to raise issues of general fire safety, on which successive governments had been dragging their heels, they were ignored. In 1985, the then minister for the environment, Liam Kavanagh, told the Dáil that he could not respond to their pleas to fully implement the Stardust tribunal recommendations, saying that "I have to be sure that any correspondence between me and any member of the victims will not be used as some sort of evidence in court cases which may occur." This prompted no less a personage than Charles Haughey to shout at him: "you are a disgrace". What has been most pointed during this 25th anniversary week of the Stardust is the extent to which we as a society are again being asked to face up to our past failures. In recent years, this has happened in a number of areas, and we have shown a willingness to accept that people have been betrayed.

It may have taken too long, but victims of the 1974 Dublin and Monaghan bombings are no longer being ignored in their search for answers. Survivors of abuse as children in State institutions are similarly being listened to, as are those affected by the actions of Dr Michael Neary at Our Lady of Lourdes Hospital in Drogheda.

The Stardust victims and relatives are simply asking that this new-found openness to re-examine the past be extended to their cause. They have ploughed years of work into a painstaking analysis of what happened that Valentine's night, and have made a compelling case that, in the interests of justice, the inquiry should be reopened. There can be no "moving on" until this happens.

# A wide boy who got off lightly
*March 23, 2006*

We wanted to know if it was libellous to call someone a brat. Legal brains pondered the matter. The conclusion eventually was that when applied to Patrick Gallagher, who died last week, it was a fair and accurate description. We could proceed. It was March 1982, and it had been the then features editor Colm Tóibín's idea to plaster the headline "Patrick Gallagher, Property Speculator and Brat" across the cover of In Dublin magazine. I was writing the article, a sorry tale of Gallagher's destruction of swathes of the city, but it was the headline which made the impact.

Patrick Gallagher had declined to be interviewed for the piece, but afterwards decided he did want to talk to me. I was summoned to a surreal evening in one of the large snugs of Ryan's in Parkgate Street, where Gallagher was ensconced with business cronies and family members. Between sessions of climbing on tables and singing loudly, he wanted to know why we had called him a brat. He wasn't a brat, he said, and wanted us to take it back. Since he then immediately burst into song again, it was difficult to take him seriously. However, there was nothing surreal about what Patrick Gallagher was doing to the capital city. Then just 30 years old, he had used it as his personal playground for the previous eight years and he was one of those children who liked smashing their toys.

The story of the Gallagher family is a parable of modern Ireland. The patriarch Matt was one of the great financial backers of Fianna Fáil. From rural stock in Sligo, he was one of the great wave of emigrants to the building sites of Britain during the 1940s. He returned in the late 1950s, with enough money to capitalise on the nascent building boom, as Ireland under Seán Lemass began to open up the economy. Matt built homes for the emerging middle classes, developing the Gallagher Group into the largest house-builders in the land. Hand and glove with Fianna Fáil, he constructed whole suburbs. There was an absolute belief that what was good for business was good for the country, which in turn was good for Fianna Fáil. It was a small world. Des Traynor, infamous now as Charles Haughey's accountant, was a director of the Gallagher Group. The seeds of subsequent scandals were already there, with the ownership of the company transferred in the early 1960s to an impenetrable parent company registered off-shore in the Cayman Islands.

But where Matt's business was to build, his son Patrick preferred to destroy. On the death of his father in 1974, Patrick radically shifted direction. The oil crisis was biting and recession was on the way. Cynical and hard-headed, Patrick sold off swathes of the Gallagher land bank in what he called "the less prestigious areas". He scaled down the building operation and concentrated on the wealthier end of the market. "We felt that in any recession there were people who would make it through," he explained. "This time they were the civil servants, the accountants, airline people and so on. We simply catered for them." It was not long, though, before Patrick realised that you didn't need to actually build anything at all in order to make money. You could buy city centre sites, demolish the fusty old buildings and sell them on. Never mind that rubble and years of dereliction replaced several of the finest examples anywhere of 19th century architecture.

As Patrick played Monopoly with Dublin streets, making vast money and flaunting it ostentatiously, it later transpired that he had also been engaging in extensive fraud. The Gallagher Group had over-extended itself. In May 1982, the banks foreclosed and everything went bust. Liquidator Paddy Shortall was appointed to examine the affairs of Merchant Banking Ltd, a Gallagher-owned bank. He discovered a series of apparently fraudulent transactions involving Patrick's use of depositors' savings to prop up his speculative empire. The liquidator identified evidence for a total of 79 possible criminal offences under six different acts. It has always remained one of the great mysteries as to why Gallagher was never even prosecuted, let alone found guilty, for any of these. The authorities in Northern Ireland, where he had a branch of his bank, did pursue him and locked him up for two years. However, his Northern operation constituted only a fraction of his activities.

Given the scale of Gallagher's apparent fraud, he must have been convinced that he was untouchable, that the normal rules and laws simply did not apply to him. It is likely that such a belief was bolstered by his close connections to the then Taoiseach Charles Haughey. After kindly providing him with an enormous gift of £300,000, Gallagher could be forgiven for believing he had the power of the land in his pocket. There has been much talk this past week in the wake of Patrick Gallagher's untimely death of Greek tragedy, of Icarus and his burning wings. The more mundane truth is that Gallagher was a wide boy with powerful friends, who in this country never had to pay for his crimes.

# Let's undo this sin of the past
*April 20, 2006*

There is a unique piece of Irish history located somewhere in Miami. Its loss to this country is a tale of nasty suppression culminating in callous indifference. This Eastertime, rather than watching weaponry jaunting through the capital city, the Government might more usefully have applied itself to undoing the shameful injustice that now deprives us of this history.

The story begins, somewhat ironically, with one of the first acts of generosity by the young Irish Free State. Taking its place among the nations of the world in the 1920s, the Irish government was enthusiastic about presenting a gift to the new League of Nations building for the headquarters of the International Labour Office in Geneva. With great imagination, the Cumann na nGaedheal government decided in 1926 to commission stained glass artist Harry Clarke to design a window for the Geneva building. Clarke had at the time an international reputation for his church windows, and the bulk of his work was religiously themed. However, for the Geneva window, he was given complete artistic freedom and clearly revelled in his liberation. He decided to create eight panels based on selected works by 15 major Irish literary figures.

WB Yeats was, according to Clarke, "wildly enthusiastic and was of tremendous help with his suggestions". Among the authors chosen to have their work represented in the window were Yeats himself, James Joyce, Sean O'Casey, James Stephens, AE, Liam O'Flaherty, GB Shaw, JM Synge, Lady Gregory, Pádraic Colum and Lennox Robinson. It was not an entirely safe subject to choose. With the Censorship of Publications Act coming into force in 1929, several of Clarke's chosen writers were about to be banned in their native land. Some had already achieved the status of pariah. Clarke was wise to this, according to an article by his son, Michael, in the catalogue for the 1988 London exhibition of his father's work. In the case of James Joyce, for instance, Harry carefully chose an early and inoffensive poem. For Liam O'Flaherty, however, he was not so circumspect.

The O'Flaherty panel caused consternation among government ministers when they finally saw the finished work. It was based on his highly successful 1926 novel, Mr Gilhooley, which had been described by WB Yeats as "a great novel". Art historian Nicola Gordon Bowe describes the panel as showing a wart-faced Gilhooley, his fat body slumped in an armchair, ogling the almost naked form of a siren draped in a translucent veil. It did not, however, appear to be the nakedness

93

which gave offence. Rather it was the fact that O'Flaherty had been included in the first place. He was a sometimes savage critic of conservative Ireland, had fought on the anti-treaty side in the Civil War and had become a communist.

The file on the fate of the Geneva window, which is to be found in the National Archives, contains an exchange of letters between Taoiseach WT Cosgrave and Clarke. On viewing the completed window at Clarke's Dublin workshop in September 1930, Cosgrave wrote to Clarke: "I consider that it would not be desirable to include the panel which contains representation from the books of Mr Liam O'Flaherty." Cosgrave hastened to add that he did not dispute the artistic merit of the piece, which he described as "a most remarkable and successful artistic achievement". His difficulty, he wrote, arose from "the fact that the inclusion of scenes from certain authors as representative of Irish literature and culture would give grave offence to many of our people". Other notes in the National Archives file indicate that the inclusion of James Joyce was also a subject of concern. Later speculation even blamed the presence of a bottle of Guinness beside the figure of Sean O'Casey's Joxer Daly.

Harry Clarke thanked the Taoiseach for his letter, the contents of which "surprise and worry me very much". The artist was by then dying of tuberculosis. Although the State had spurned the window, even refusing to put it on public display, Clarke was eventually paid for his work. The check for £450 arrived three weeks after his death in January 1931. He was 41. The government then set about "disposing" of the window. Two years later, they arranged for Clarke's widow, Margaret, to buy it back - it cost her £450. This, of course, was now a Fianna Fáil government, but nothing had changed. The Clarke family allowed the window to go on display at the Hugh Lane gallery during the 1970s, but in 1988 they decided to sell it. There appeared to be no interest from the State. It was bought for a six-figure sum by the Wolfsonian Foundation in Florida, where it now resides.

The fate of the Geneva window encapsulates what this country became on foot of the 1916 Rising - narrow, mean-spirited and dishonourable. It is easy to wallow in sentimentality and smug notions of inclusiveness, celebrating the aspirations of the Proclamation and parading around the place with big guns. It is more uncomfortable, but profoundly more worthwhile, to set right the sins of the past. It is time to bring the Geneva window home.

# Children on losing side again

*June 8, 2006*

It is apparently all our own fault that children are now going to be torn apart in court during cross-examination. In galloping the Criminal Law (Sexual Offences) Act 2006 through the Oireachtas, the tone of the Minister for Justice was decidedly petulant. What has transpired - namely the exposure of already traumatised children to the further abuse of cross-examination - is not what the public wanted. That this should be the upshot of a frenzied few weeks in the Dáil and at the courts is a dismal reflection on both. Despite the self-serving pronouncements of Michael McDowell, it is not necessary to have children brutalised by the courts. It is generally a matter for each judge to ensure that the cross-examination of anyone, and particularly of vulnerable children, should not exceed reasonable limits. The question obviously arises as to how those limits should be defined. In this area, judges at present have little to guide them.

The Constitution is clear about the right of an accused person to a fair trial (including the right to examine his accuser). However, it is essentially silent on the rights of children. Consequently, in adjudicating on the balance of rights in this area, the absence of constitutional protection for the welfare of the child will invariably mean that the rights of the adult (in this case, a person accused of child rape) will take clear precedence. What is required as a matter of urgency is that this balance should be redressed. To do so requires the introduction of an amendment to the Constitution enshrining the paramount importance of children's welfare. This view is expressed strongly by constitutional lawyer Geoffrey Shannon, who has produced a number of reports on the area. Just yesterday, he addressed a session of the UN Committee on the Rights of the Child. This committee is currently examining how Ireland is facing up to its responsibilities on children's rights. It also heard a submission from Children's Ombudsman Emily Logan. "What happened last week on statutory rape makes the argument for an urgent constitutional amendment on child protection even more compelling," Geoffrey Shannon told me yesterday. "If you allow rigorous cross-examination of children, it means that they will be re-victimised. The current Supreme Court has veered away from enumerating the rights of the child, holding that this is the responsibility of government. In this context, the only way forward is through proper constitutional protection for children." Geoffrey Shannon acknowledges some advances have been made, particularly by Minister of State for Children Brian Lenihan. However, on the constitutional front, it does not appear anyone in the Dáil is all that interested.

# Children on losing side again

The issue first came to prominence 13 years ago in the report on the F incest case by Catherine McGuinness, now a Supreme Court judge. She recommended the Constitution be amended to include "a specific and overt declaration of the rights of born children". This was followed in 1996 by the report of the government-appointed Constitution Review Group. In probably the most detailed consideration of the issue either before or since, it pointed directly to the lack of constitutional protection for children. It recommended that the Constitution be amended, and suggested a specific wording, taken from the UN Convention on the Rights of the Child: "In all actions concerning children, whether undertaken by public or private social welfare institutions, courts of law, administrative authorities or legislative bodies, the best interests of the child shall be of paramount consideration." A decade (and several more reports) later, nothing has happened. Even worse, the All-Party Oireachtas Committee on the Constitution has now substantially rowed back on the recommendations made 10 years previously.

Reporting last January, this committee agreed that a constitutional amendment was required but suggested a different and considerably weaker wording: "In all cases where the welfare of the child so requires, regard shall be had to the best interests of that child." There is a yawning legal chasm between a provision which makes the best interests of the child of "paramount consideration", and a vague statement that "regard shall be had" to them. Geoffrey Shannon was horrified by this change in attitude by the Oireachtas. It is a matter which he raised yesterday at the UN hearings. "I would despair if this is the collected wisdom of all the parties in the Dáil," he told me. "It's deeply disappointing that they should be going backwards, particularly after all the tribunals and inquiries we have had into child abuse. How many more will we need before we finally put in place proper constitutional protection for children?" Perhaps all of those concerned and committed citizens who rang radio programmes and gathered to protest last week might turn their attention in a concrete way to campaign for a referendum to amend the Constitution.

# National day of hypocrisy

*June 15, 2006*

It is tempting to ease into the soft, squishy space that is nostalgia. When combined, as it was last Tuesday, with an understandably decent instinct not to speak ill of the dead, it produced something akin to a national day of hypocrisy. Charlie Haughey, himself a master of that particular trait, would have been proud of us, while laughing up his sleeve. As the hours lengthened after his death, there was a palpable sense both in the Dáil and on the airwaves that no one wanted to be the first to spoil the mood, even if it meant telling the truth.

In serious injury cases, doctors speak of the critical importance of the first hour of treatment. In politics, the equivalent is perhaps 24 hours - whoever controls that period can set the tone. As the great and the good fell over themselves to pay tribute to a man who narrowly avoided being sent to jail for stealing from the Irish people, it became clear that there were four main points they wished to stitch into the public psyche: Charlie founded the Celtic Tiger; he initiated the peace process; he was kind and generous; he was cultured and intelligent.

He was himself intensely concerned with his own public image. I first came across him in the course of my work as a producer on RTÉ's current affairs series Today Tonight. I had been assigned to cover the 1986 Fianna Fáil Ardfheis, a crucial one for the party as it was to be the last before the 1987 general election. I was summoned to the royal presence. Charlie shook my hand and, without speaking, clicked his fingers. The door opened and in paraded a line of people carrying an assortment of suits, ties and shirts. "Take her in there," barked The Boss, "and get her to pick out what I should wear for the speech." The leader's speech was to be broadcast live for an hour at prime time the following evening. Bemused, I meekly trotted after the row of human clothes-hangers. PJ Mara, the voce at the time for his Duce, pressed me for a decision. The extraordinary assumption that I, as an RTÉ journalist, was there to provide advice as to how to make the Fianna Fáil leader look good on television was profoundly revealing of the party's attitude to the national broadcaster. Together with everything else in the country, they considered that they owned it.

I had already done battle with various Haughey minions that week. RTÉ's approach to covering ardfheiseanna was that cameras shooting speakers were set at their eye-level. To film people from above invariably serves to diminish them visually. To shoot them from below makes them appear larger and more dominant.

(Mussolini's insistence on always being shot from a low angle was no accident.) Eye-level coverage is the only fair and impartial option. This, however, cut no ice with Fianna Fáil. They had arranged an enormous photograph of Haughey as a backdrop to the stage. The party handlers were determined that the main camera covering Charlie should be at a low angle, to set him magisterially against the vast image of himself behind. They appeared to have cast me as some form of latter-day Leni Riefenstahl. Every time my back was turned, the platform holding the camera opposite the podium would have mysteriously reduced in size. I'd instruct the riggers to build it back up to its proper height, and again a few hours later, it would have shrunk. Meanwhile, I was being pressed for an answer about the Duce's tie - difficult enough, as all were sleek and gorgeous. Cornered, I chose the colour least suited to someone of Haughey's determined character. That one, I said, pointing to a pink contraption. Shrewd as always, Charlie wore blue.

On becoming Taoiseach again in 1987, he flexed his muscles across the land. RTÉ was targeted, with its advertising revenue capped to facilitate the creation of competitors. Haughey's message was clear and was understood: I am in control; cause me any trouble and I'll punish you further. It was against this backdrop, in 1989, that we in Today Tonight unearthed documentary evidence that property tycoon Patrick Gallagher had given money to Haughey, illegally using depositors' funds from the bank he [Gallagher] owned. When asked to comment, Haughey indicated in the most forceful manner that he had in his back pocket a writ which he would serve on RTÉ if we even hinted at the matter. RTÉ ruled that we should exclude all reference to money handed out to Haughey by Gallagher from our programme exposing the latter's fraudulent activities. While this decision was certainly informed by legal advice, I personally have no doubt that it was also influenced by the climate of fear for the future of the public broadcaster which Haughey had so directly engineered.

Thanks to the tribunals, we now know that Patrick Gallagher was only one of several shelling out vast sums to their best pal Charlie. In 1989, this was not public knowledge. Through threat and intimidation, the soldier of destiny in his Charvet shirt had managed for a while longer to hide the source of his wealth.

# Hey presto, PDs get rid of problems
*July 6, 2006*

It's a good trick, if you can manage it. It presupposes a certain doziness on the part of the general population, a criterion which we in this country appear eminently capable of satisfying. The question was how to reduce hospital waiting lists.

These had been a major bugbear for successive governments, and had even been credited with losing Fianna Fáil an election or two. The solution was bold and imaginative. Simply stop recording them. If nobody counts them, then they cannot be reported. They will have vanished. Hey presto! No more waiting lists in the new Irish health utopia. Breda O'Gorman should really be told this. The fact that she has had to wait over six months for an operation to control the extreme pain which she suffers as a result of her multiple sclerosis is clearly an illusion. What she needs is a simple procedure to insert a pump which will deliver pain killers to the appropriate site. She will then be able to receive physiotherapy. Since Christmas, the agony has been too severe to allow even this, and Breda is deteriorating fast. The 3,133 children waiting for a psychiatric assessment - assessment, mind you, not even treatment - should know better. Some of them have been waiting for up to two years. But, of course, they are not really on a waiting list.

We don't do waiting lists in Ireland any more. Those waiting for rehabilitation services, 245 at the most recent count, some of them for up to three years, will doubtless be cheered by Mary Harney's recent statements that our long waiting lists have gone away. Likewise for the 200 patients awaiting urgent neurosurgery treatment, some of who are critically ill. Similar patterns exist for orthopaedic procedures and for cancer treatments. Last week's European Health Consumer Index report, produced by a Swedish-based organisation, looked for a while as if it might burst our happy little bubble. It compared a range of consumer-oriented health indicators across the EU. Incomprehensibly, Ireland came out second worst. Thankfully, Mary Harney was able to clear up the matter for us. The figures used in the EHCI report were all out of date, she explained. They clearly came from a time when we used to record silly things like waiting lists. Don't these Swedes understand that now that we've stopped doing this, everything is much better? The Minister for Health tells us that these days no one in Ireland waits for longer than three months. The brilliant new National Treatment Purchase Fund sees to this. It is an ingenious mechanism of funnelling public money into private hospitals to allow patients to be treated there at the taxpayers' expense. God forbid that we should use the money to invest in our public hospitals. When we did that, we used to have waiting lists, after all. Incidentally, this same National Treatment Purchase Fund is also the body charged with drawing up overall national statistics on waiting lists. But since we don't have any, it of course does not waste its time doing this. It simply chirrups away about what a great job it does.

By highly convoluted and elaborate extrapolations of what paltry figures have managed to survive the cull, it has been estimated that, in reality, over 29,000 patients are on waiting lists for hospital treatment in this country. But we have no way anymore of knowing how long people have been waiting, or how many people die untreated. Just like we are not allowed know how many people die of MRSA. Officially, no one really does. They die of other things, or of the great catch-all known as "complications". The innovative approach to solving the problem of hospital waiting lists by the simple expedient of ceasing to record them, is a measure we are likely to see expanded to other areas as a general election approaches. But there is no reason to confine the success of such a brilliant measure to health alone.

It is surprising that no one has thought of this before. And it is no accident that we have the Progressive Democrats, the brainiest party in Ireland, to thank for it. We know already, for instance, that in the Department of Justice they have attempted something similar by playing fast and loose with the mechanisms for accumulating crime figures. They should really cut out pussy-footing about and just stop recording crime altogether. Then we wouldn't have a problem, would we? Pollution could vanish in a similar way, carbon emissions would become a thing of the past, a distant memory of the bad old days when we foolishly measured these phenomena. Climate change would merely mean Ireland becoming a sun destination for foreign tourists. Poverty also would no longer be with us. Nor would obesity or diabetes. But why stop there? Why not abolish death itself? The possibilities are endless. Why have we never thought of this before? In truth, we must all really be dozy. Except for the PDs, of course.

# How do you define terrorism
*July 20, 2006*

I once spent five hours being shelled by the Israeli Defence Forces. It was during the mid-1990s and, unlike most of the Lebanese population during the past week, I felt relatively safe. I had the protection of Unifil, the UN peace-keeping force in south Lebanon, and was sheltering in one of the bunkers of the Irish battalion.

What had happened was part of everyday life in south Lebanon, which had been repeatedly invaded and occupied by Israel over the previous decades. I was there to film for RTÉ the impact on the ground of Unifil and the Irish Army. We were due to observe the routine protection given to local farmers tending their crops. Without this, farmers were regularly attacked and killed by either the Israeli Defence Forces (IDF) or their surrogates in the region. That morning, the Irish patrol and our film crew were due to meet the farmers at 5.30am. At 5am, the IDF began its attack, extensively bombing a wide area which included our farmers' fields. While we sat safe in our bunker, people were being killed and maimed during that five hours of indiscriminate shelling of ordinary Lebanese all around us.

The excuse provided by the Israelis was as familiar then as it is now. They had a right to defend themselves against Hizbullah rocket attacks and would do whatever it took to fight for their own security. The concept of disproportionate response was equally familiar. During one six-month period in the 1990s, for instance, the UN recorded over 16,000 artillery, mortar and tank rounds fired by the Israelis in Lebanon, a number of which were targeted directly at villages, killing and mutilating scores of local people. Over the same period, Hizbullah mounted 87 attacks, overwhelmingly against the military target of the Israeli forces. Irish battalion figures showed that, for a similar six-month period in 1995 - neither better nor worse than most during the 1990s - Irish troops, as part of Unifil, came under direct Israeli attack on 61 occasions. This compared with six attacks mounted by Hizbullah against northern Israel during the same period.

The importance of the Irish and UN presence in Lebanon was as much to bear witness to atrocity as to secure any particular military objective. While the UN mandate specified as its aim the withdrawal of the Israeli occupying forces from south Lebanon, everyone knew that this was simply unrealistic. Much as it is now similarly unrealistic to expect the Lebanese army to swoop on Hizbullah and disarm them. Unifil was keenly aware that its main usefulness was in attempting to prevent Israel from enlarging its area of occupation. Through trying to contain Israel, the hope was that Lebanese civilians might be provided with some degree of safety. The mission was often hopelessly ineffectual, as people continued to be killed and the IDF drove straight through Unifil on a number of occasions. But the mission did represent an important statement by the international community that bullying, aggression, unlawful occupation and the bombing of civilians was wrong. And this is perhaps one of the more disturbing aspects of the current slaughter by Israel of Lebanese people - the unwillingness, perhaps the inability, of that same international community to recognise any more actions that are simply wrong and to condemn them as such. It is, of course, equally wrong that any group, be it Hizbullah or Hamas, should target and kill Israeli citizens. We have no difficulty condemning this in unequivocal and unambiguous terms as terrorism.

But terrorism, according to the Oxford English Dictionary, is defined as "a policy intended to strike with terror those against whom it is adopted", a description which neatly sums up Israeli activity in both Lebanon and Gaza. Bombing civilian populations back to the Middle Ages, to a condition where they have no electricity, no water, no sewerage, no fuel, no roads, no vehicles and are running out of food certainly qualifies as an act of state terrorism. Part of the reason why the international community, led by the US, has such difficulty in recognising this was provided by an analysis of Israeli and Jewish power within the US administration. Undertaken by two leading American academics earlier this year, it identified the power and wealth of the Israel lobby at the heart of US politics. The authors, Prof Stephen Walt, dean of the John F. Kennedy School of Government at Harvard, and Prof John Mearsheimer, of the University of Chicago, were roundly attacked for daring to raise such a taboo subject. As with anyone who has the temerity to criticise Israel, they were accused of bigotry and anti-Semitism. For their part, they had pointed to the de facto control by Israel of US public opinion. Media commentary on the Middle East, they contended, was starkly unbalanced in overwhelmingly favouring Israel.

In Europe, we do not have the excuse that the powers that be keep us in ignorance of the atrocious reality of Israel's activities in Lebanon and Gaza. Each one of us has an obligation to speak out in the face of such palpable wrong.

# Annual fleecing of parents

*August 10, 2006*

John is 15 and has just finished his Junior Cert. His 12-year-old sister Ciara is about to go into secondary school. Their parents were hoping that Ciara could inherit all of John's school books, which even after three years' use remain in good condition. They reckoned this would save them almost €400. But it was not to be. Ciara, who is going to the local convent, girls-only school, was sent her book list during the summer. To her parents' horror, not a single one of her brother's books appeared on that list. They could not understand it - the subjects were the same, the curriculums identical. The nasty reality for parents is that there are no single, standardised texts for secondary school subjects, or even at primary level. There is a vast array of books to choose from, and that choice is made by the teacher.

John and Ciara's parents must shell out for a completely different set of books for Ciara, covering precisely the same curriculum as that already studied by her brother.
And this is not the first time it has happened to them. While both their children attended the same national school, they each had to have different books. Teachers have their own preferences, and the books for one year's fourth class, for example, can change completely the following year, when a new teacher takes over. Some schools sensibly standardise their texts so that siblings can inherit books, but others allow the teachers free choice. There is yet another snag, even with the same books used each year. Some of them have a few pages at the back in which the pupils are expected to write answers. These consequently are no longer suitable to be passed on to other children. This kind of built-in obsolescence ensures continuing healthy profits for the publishers of school books. Not surprisingly, John and Ciara's parents can't help feeling that they are being ripped off. While one might argue that competition and choice should operate in the interests of consumers in this area, it is clear that in many instances the opposite is the case. Most of the books in each subject are roughly the same price. Take Junior Cert history for example: there are at least five different texts, all costing €25 to €35. Presentation, style and illustration vary, but the content is virtually identical as each book must follow the standard course set by the Department of Education. Beleaguered parents, paying up to €1,350 on books and uniforms for a child at secondary school, according to this week's Labour Party survey, must wonder why it is not possible to produce a single text in each subject, centrally printed, distributed to the schools, there to be bought by the pupils. With the huge economy of scale involved here - a captive market of around 800,000 school-going children - this must inevitably result in

substantial savings across the board, not least by the elimination of the middle layer of bookshops. This is not in any way to advocate the production of dull, utilitarian state texts. There is no earthly reason why lively, vibrant, colourful school books could not be produced centrally by panels of experienced teachers, and even involve the students themselves in their design. With the availability these days of extensive internet resources, it is no longer convincing to argue (as in the past) that competition in school texts is necessary to provide diversity of choice.

The State's solution to the crisis faced by parents unable to afford the costs of books and uniforms is to provide a grant. It has never shown any inclination to interfere with the highly lucrative free market in school texts, worth up to €60 million a year and growing consistently at well over the rate of inflation. The grant itself operates as a prop to this private market, and given its low income threshold does not even assist many of those who desperately need it. Book rental schemes may certainly help, but with the wholly unregulated nature of the market, they can be cumbersome and difficult to organise. There is a clear case here for direct intervention from government, for a bit of public initiative, rather than slavishly allowing the free market and private enterprise to rule. It is surely at the very least worthwhile investigating the kind of savings to parents which the production of a single, standardised textbook for each subject might entail. And while they are at it, why not also look into the idea of having a standard school uniform as well? The costs in some cases for fancy blazers and specialised sportswear are truly scandalous, and can apply in both fee-paying and so-called free schools equally. Individual parents have little choice but to swallow hard and buy whatever their child's school demands. Collectively, however, they have the potential to wield enormous clout. That they should organise to use this power to put a halt to their annual fleecing seems to be a no-brainer.

# A State-run house of horrors
*August 17, 2006*

If you put television cameras into this place, the nation would be shocked to its core.

Among the events recorded, some of which involve children as young as 10, would have been the following: an older child repeatedly bashing a smaller one's head off a kitchen press; persistent self-harm by children, together with stated intentions to commit suicide; an assault by two youngsters on a third boy, following which the victim himself was punished; a total of at least 44 separate incidents of violence and aggression - and all this over a three-month period from March to May of this year.

This house of horrors is a State-run children's home. It is supposed to provide safety and sanctuary for those youngsters who, for reasons of abuse or neglect, the State has removed from their own families and taken into care. These are the most vulnerable of children, deeply traumatised and behaving accordingly, suffering from a range of disabilities, primary among which is the absence of a family who can look after them. They are reliant on the State for their very existence. Figures produced this week indicate that in 2004, more than 5,000 children were being cared for by the State. Some of them end up in centres such as the one mentioned above, which caters for up to four children and is run by the HSE. It is in southwest Dublin, and we know about it as a result of a report published this month by the Social Services Inspectorate. While the centre is not named, it is clear that it has been the subject of concern for a number of years.

In 2000, the inspectorate made a total of 44 recommendations for improvement. By 2005, only 14 had been fully implemented, eight partially implemented and 22 had been completely ignored. The inspectorate made 34 additional recommendations and said it would visit the home again in 2006. When the inspection team returned in early June of this year, they began assessing the implementation of these recommendations.

However, they state in their report that "it quickly became apparent during the inspection fieldwork that there were grave concerns for the safety and welfare of the young people in the centre". The home was badly managed, they concluded. It had an enormous turnover of staff, with up to 50 individuals having worked there on and off over the previous six months. Many of them were agency staff, completely unknown to the children.

One boy, whose home had been the centre for five years, was "discharged" with no event or party to mark his departure and no indication as to when he might see his younger brother again. There had been no consideration of the emotional impact involved in the separation of the two siblings. Two of the children had threatened to commit suicide, and one was engaged in serious self-harm. The children had complained about their bedrooms being cold and having to sleep on urine-soaked mattresses. They had repeatedly told people how unhappy they were. Their complaints were not taken seriously. A number of staff members had also complained, including some of the agency workers. There was equally little evidence that their concerns had been acted on. The Social Services Inspectorate recommended that the home be shut down and the children relocated. Its report concluded that "the young people were living in an emotionally impoverished and unpredictable environment in a centre that was intended to be their home. "The experience for the young people was that their medical needs were not met, their education was disrupted, family visits were cancelled, they were subject to inappropriate practice and discontinuities in their placements, there were many occasions when strangers were their sole carers and they were repeatedly exposed to violence and aggression."

The HSE is now moving to find alternative accommodation for the children at this centre, and anticipates that it will be closed within weeks. Further, it must be said that most children in care do not live in such a climate.

According to a range of inspectorate reports over the years, a number of HSE-run children's homes provide good, stable care, with warm and caring relations between staff and children. However, there is a pattern in several homes of inadequate provision and of recommendations not being implemented. For instance, the inspectorate pointed earlier this year to increasing evidence of medication being used to control the behaviour of children in some care homes, and instanced one centre where physical restraints were inappropriately used in a routine manner, causing actual harm to the children. These kinds of incidents, and the years of inaction at the care home described above, seriously challenge the effectiveness of the State's child protection mechanisms. Combined with reports this week that only 40 per cent of the 6,000 reports of child abuse made in 2004 have so far been fully investigated, the picture for vulnerable children in this country is profoundly grim.

# Jordan's juggling act a success
*September 7, 2006*

The happy couple squeezed into the hotel through the security metal detector to the accompaniment of traditional chanting and drum-beating from the wedding guests. The bride entered on one side of the swimming pool, the groom on the other. As they met on a little ornamental bridge over the pool, fireworks whizzed, video cameras rolled, and they chastely kissed. To the booming soundtrack of Whitney Houston's I Will Always Love You , they danced on the bridge amidst clouds of dry ice. It was an ordinary, everyday, Muslim wedding last week in a hotel in Amman, the capital of Jordan, where I happened to be staying briefly while on holiday. As Whitney Houston concluded, the beaming couple took up occupation of a white, throne-like couch, and presided over the enthusiastic dancing of their guests to the distinctive Arabic music of the Middle East. (There was of course not a drop of alcohol in sight for the entire evening.) This easy musical symbiosis of East and West seemed entirely natural to the wedding party. It is a reflection of the relatively laid-back attitude of Jordanians to all sorts of outside influences - an approach which has characterised this remarkable country for thousands of years.

Consequently, the news last Monday that elsewhere in Amman a lone gunman opened fire on a group of western tourists, killing one UK national and injuring a number of others, came as a shock. For westerners, wandering around Amman and elsewhere in Jordan, there is no sense of threat or hostility. What you hear most often is a heartfelt "ahlan wa sahlan", the Jordanian equivalent of a hundred-thousand welcomes. All of which is of course cold comfort to the family of Chris Stokes, shot dead in Amman on Monday. He was an accountant from Manchester, who had spent the past few years working in Ireland. Although the gunman clearly targeted a group of westerners and shouted "Allahu akbar" (God is great) as he opened fire, it appears at this stage that he was acting alone rather than as part of any terrorist organisation. Tony Blair, in condemning the shooting, attempted to link it to the killings the same day of British troops in Iraq and Afghanistan, emphasising again his world view of a global threat to the West from Islamic fundamentalism. The lumping together of all such incidents into an all-embracing concept of "axis of evil" assaults on westerners by Muslims serves to fuel a dangerously divisive paranoia.

Take Jordan, for instance. Although a Muslim country, it contains a number of shades of political opinion, from the pro-Western King Abdullah II and his government, to more fundamentalist Islamic groups which have strong support among the urban population, many of whom are of Palestinian origin. It remains, however, one of the most stable and peaceful countries in the Middle East. The Islamists condemn the use of violence for political ends just as strongly as the government, as was clear from the local response of outrage to al-Qaeda's attack on Amman last year, when over 60 people, mainly Jordanians, were killed in three suicide bombings of hotels. Widely viewed as Jordan's 9/11, it was a rare act of terrorism on Jordanian soil. The country has been described as being quite literally between Iraq and a hard place - namely Israel - and it also shares borders with Syria, the West Bank and Saudi Arabia. Despite the animosity between a number of its neighbours, Jordan has managed to remain on friendly terms with all of them. It is a high-wire balancing act of awesome proportions when one considers that the country has taken in well over a million refugees from Palestine, Iraq and, most recently, Lebanon. The former king, Hussein, made peace with Israel in the mid-1990s. Although significantly strained by the attack on Lebanon, cordial relations with Israel have been maintained by his son and successor, Abdullah, whose cherubic countenance stares out from shops and cafes throughout the country. Jordan and Israel now have plans to co-operate on a range of economic ventures, including the saving of the Dead Sea which is in danger of drying up completely in just over 40 years' time.

There is a strong sense that Jordanians are proud of their political moderation and their ability to make and keep the peace with Israel, which not even considerable public anger at the assault on Lebanon managed to derail. Which is not to say that they don't have their problems. Threats to destabilise the country are ever-present. It has no large natural resources of its own, has a serious water shortage and an unemployment rate which is estimated at 30 per cent. While the king and the government are pursuing a "national agenda" to increase personal freedoms, human rights abuses, particularly the use of torture by the security police, remain a serious concern of the UN. Nonetheless, the overwhelming impression from the streets and arid desert landscapes of Jordan is of a people managing to survive as honestly as they can amid the power struggles which surround them on all sides.

# In danger of a siege mentality
*September 14, 2006*

It has been argued that in 1956 we did not know any better, that our ignorance, prejudice and xenophobia were not our fault. Rather they were an inevitable consequence of the highly insular society which prevailed at the time.

This year marks the fiftieth anniversary of the Soviet invasion of Hungary. The Irish government - in 1956 it was Fianna Fáil - was keen to prove to the world that it could do its bit, and took in its quota of refugees (530 of them) fleeing Hungary in fear of their lives. Irish compassion, however, did not stretch to non-Catholics - there was an insistence that only RC Hungarians be allowed on to our hallowed isle. Things went well at first. Crowds cheered the first arrivals at Shannon airport. We were delighted to be delivering them from godless communism. The fact that they were shunted into a disused army camp at Knockalisheen in Co Clare, a bleak and isolated barracks, did not unduly concern us. We had done our duty, had rescued refugees in accordance with our new-found international obligations, and they should be grateful. They weren't a bit grateful, of course. They complained about the bad food, the freezing barracks, the fact that they felt virtually imprisoned there, and that they could not work. They were labouring people, they said, and all they wanted was to be able to earn an honest living.

Eventually, after months of isolation, they went on hunger strike. The general view of this was that they should shut up and behave themselves. Fianna Fáil's Donogh O'Malley appeared particularly annoyed, thundering in the Dail that the Hungarians should be told "that while they are living in this country they will have to behave themselves in a reasonable manner." Other TDs asked were "our own people not entitled to any jobs that are going?" Fine Gael's Bill Murphy could have taken a leaf out of Marie Antoinette's book with his comment that he would happily allow the Hungarians to strike. "We have a lot of people who have not got rashers and eggs for their breakfast but these people have got them." It was Taoiseach Eamon de Valera who attempted to moderate the debate by reminding deputies that "we have not passed through the trials which they have." Desperate to leave a country which had treated them so badly, most of the Hungarian refugees were eventually re-settled in Canada.

One wonders what de Valera might have thought of events in Tralee last week, when a group of 60 refugees again went on hunger strike in this country. Living at the Atlas House hostel, they were complaining about the food, often undercooked and inedible they claimed, and also about restrictions on visitors and activities.

# In danger of a siege mentality

They are not allowed to work and their entire income consists of the €19.10 they receive under direct provision. Some of them have lived like this for several years. Much like the Hungarians, it was only through the extreme action of refusing to eat that they could get anyone to take their problems seriously. The complaints of poor facilities, food and treatment in asylum hostels are by no means confined to Atlas House. With so little personal money at their disposal, asylum seekers in Ireland are wholly dependent on the hostels where they live and are acutely vulnerable to abuse.

It is somewhat ironic then that this week should also have seen us initiated into the mysteries of Operation Gull, designed to target social welfare fraud committed by foreign nationals. It was reported by this newspaper that (unnamed) sources close to the investigation were "staggered" by the level of abuses uncovered. And the amounts of money involved in these shocking crimes? Over the two years of Operation Gull, it is estimated at €6.6 million. Certainly a substantial sum, but what was not mentioned was that it represents something less than one percent of the €800 million total fraud within the social welfare system for the same period. This of course is fraud perpetrated almost entirely by Irish people. While it is always valid to highlight fraud, whoever commits it, it will be interesting to see how the current attention on foreigners in this regard will play into the wider political agenda. The Minister for Justice has introduced his new Bill to force non-EU citizens to carry ID cards with biometric data, and to permit the immediate deportation of foreigners who fail to be "of good behaviour generally". And the Government will shortly have to decide whether or not to allow Bulgarians and Romanians free access to our labour market on the accession of their countries to the EU. In a climate where a recent Sunday Tribune opinion poll indicated that a sizeable majority of Irish people believe that immigration is destroying traditional Irish values (whatever they are), the dangers of encouraging a siege mentality are all too evident. Perhaps in 1956 we did indeed know no better in terms of our attitudes to others. You might think, however, in the intervening half century that we might have learned a thing or two.

# Consultants fail to make strong case
*September 21, 2006*

The last time I wrote about the proposed changes in the policing of the medical profession I was accused by the Irish Hospital Consultants' Association of having "an intense dislike of doctors". This was from Donal Duffy, of the IHCA, writing to this newspaper last month. It is a good old debating trick - deflect the argument by imputing motives of personal malice.

I must hasten to reassure the IHCA that, far from disliking doctors, I - in common with everyone else - have good reason to be grateful to them for curing my own and my family's ills. However, none of that has any bearing on the fact that many of the consultants' objections to the new Medical Practitioners Bill are plain daft. The IHCA last week produced its response to the proposed legislation. It focused on the powers of the Minister for Health to appoint the members of the new Medical Council (the body which regulates the profession) and to fire them or even dismiss the entire council. It also condemned the authority of the Minister to give general policy directions to the council. These are described as "extraordinary powers" and the IHCA warns darkly that they fly in the face of the Hippocratic oath and interfere in the doctor/patient relationship. However, what is thoroughly bizarre about the consultants' objections to these provisions is that they do not appear to have noticed that none of them is new. These "extraordinary powers" they complain of are all contained in the old Medical Practitioners Act, 1978, and have never previously incurred the wrath of the IHCA. There are some slight differences in wording. The consultants object to the power of the Minister in future to appoint the 25 members of the council. However, it is clearly specified in the new Bill that she must appoint a range of individuals either elected or nominated by particular bodies. This is almost identical to the mechanism defined by the 1978 Act, which stated that "the Minister shall take all steps necessary to secure the appointment of members" who have been either elected or nominated by specified organisations.

As to the Minister's power to remove the council from office, this has always existed. It has never arisen, and can only occur both in the 1978 Act and in the new Bill in a particular circumstance where the council is derelict in its duty. For the past three decades it has been regarded as a normal and uncontroversial provision. As far as the Minister's new power to give "general policy directions" goes, it is specified that these refer only to "the performance by the council of its functions". Of far greater significance is the provision which allows the Minister to assign additional functions to the council, but this also is not remotely new. It was contained in identical form in the 1978 Act.

There are essentially only two explanations for the strikingly spurious nature of the consultants' assault on the new Medical Practitioners Bill. The first is that they failed to notice that they have lived happily for almost 30 years with legal provisions to which they are now taking such exception. However, it is far more likely that their bluster is a calculated tactic to pressurise the Minister for Health to appoint a majority of medics to the new council. For their own reasons of political advantage, the consultants have represented the new Bill as something in the nature of a takeover of the profession by lay people.

In reality, it is no such thing. A minimum of 12 of the 25 members will be doctors. Given the complex basis of appointments, it is perfectly possible that, in fact, up to two-thirds of the members will be medical professionals. The final decision on this will lie with the Minister for Health. It is likely that the essentially meaningless sound and fury emanating from the IHCA is nothing more than a jockeying for position to maintain self-regulation for doctors. They lay great emphasis on their own competence to regulate themselves, something which was not in evidence when it came to the barbaric practices of Michael Neary, who needlessly cut the wombs out of dozens of women in Drogheda. It is worth remembering that while the Medical Council did eventually strike him off, no fewer than six of his fellow doctors had previously certified that he was perfectly fit to continue working as an obstetrician. The IHCA does, however, have a point when it questions the ability of lay people to assess complaints against doctors. There is no particular reason to suppose that the simple fact of being a non-doctor uniquely qualifies anyone for such adjudication. It is a great shame that Mary Harney did not bite the bullet and put in place a fully professional and independent medical ombudsman's office, similar to that in New Zealand, specifically geared towards the investigation of complaints and potential medical scandals. It is only through such a mechanism that public faith can be properly restored in a profession that has lately taken such a battering.

# Something rotten in Ryanair
*October 12, 2006*

There has been an analogy made in some quarters that Ryanair's bid to take over Aer Lingus represents a battle between the old and the new Ireland. Aer Lingus is predictably cast as the "old" - backward, union-ridden, inefficient, monolithic. Ryanair is the people's champion, the breaker of monopolies, forward-looking, flexible, focused on profit and proud of it. However, to those who are happy to identify with Ryanair as typifying the new Ireland, the comments of Mr Justice Thomas Smyth in the High Court during the summer might come as a sharp shock. "There are occasions," he said, "of which this is regretfully I think the second in my career as a judge I have had to do so, to say things that I found extremely difficult but which could not be left unsaid."

Ryanair had gone to the High Court alleging that pilots were being bullied and intimidated by their pro-trade union colleagues. The case was taken against the trade unions Impact, IALPA and BALPA (the Irish and British airline pilots associations). The bullying pilots were hiding behind aliases on a chat website, Ryanair claimed, and the court should order their true identities be revealed. Instead, in an unusually perfect example of being hoist by one's own petard, it was Ryanair itself which was found to be the bully.

The background is as follows: in 2004, Ryanair was in the process of switching its aircraft from Boeing 737-200s to the more up-to-date 737-800s, and pilots needed to be retrained on the newer planes. Ryanair wrote to all its pilots on November 12th, 2004, informing them that the company would refund them the training costs (€15,000) only if certain conditions were met. One of these was that should "Ryanair be compelled to engage in collective bargaining with any pilot association or trade union within five years of commencement of your conversion training, then you will be liable to repay the full training costs". The letter's next sentence is an example of the famous Ryanair cheekiness which we all, for some unfathomable reason, appear to find so endearing. The pilots were told that "naturally this does not and will not affect your right to freely join any trade union or association of your choice." Mr Justice Smyth was scathing about this. Describing it as "a Hobson's choice", he said it was "both irrational and unjust" that a pilot "through no act or default on his part could suffer the loss of €15,000". He added: "In my judgment this is a most onerous condition and bears all the hallmarks of oppression." Pilots were understandably aggrieved by this condition. Ryanair management tried to discover what they were saying to each other on their website. Apparently supplied with a password by someone described by Mr Justice Smyth variously as a traitor, informer, Iscariot or Iago, the company infiltrated the website, and then took its court action to discover the identities of pilots who signed themselves "cantfly-wontfly" and "ihateryanair". The judge found that there was no evidence of any bullying or intimidation of pilots by their colleagues on the website. He found wholly against Ryanair, and ordered the company to pay the costs of the seven-day action, estimated to be about €1 million. He specifically found that the evidence of two senior members of Ryanair staff was "baseless and false". He judged that the real purpose of the company in investigating the pilots' website "was to break whatever resolve there might have been amongst the captains to seek better terms." He further stated that the decision to involve the Garda Síochána was unwarranted and had "all the hallmarks of action in terrorem" (i.e. designed to terrify).

Mr Justice Smyth took two hours to deliver his 65-page judgment last July. His further characterisations of the actions of Ryanair include the following: "despotic indifference", "sneering disregard", "facade of concern", "unburdened by integrity". Justice Smyth concluded that "without hesitation, I find as a fact that ... 'fairness' did not seem to come into the reckoning of the plaintiff [ Ryanair] in its dealings with the defendants on the issues raised in and by this case. In summary, in the words of Isabella in Measure for Measure Act II.2: 'Oh, it is excellent to have a giant's strength; but it is tyrannous to use it like a giant'." It is important to remember that these are not the views of disgruntled Ryanair employees, or of passengers fed up by all the hidden charges on top of the airline's flight costs. It is, rather, an insight into the culture of Ryanair from an impeccably authoritative source, a judge of the land dispassionately and impartially considering the facts as laid before him.

It begs an important question. Do we really wish to equate the kind of values defined by Mr Justice Smyth with the "new" Ireland? Are we happy that a company which engages in activities so roundly condemned by the judge should stand for us as an emblem of what we wish and hope our society to become?

# Brothers should be contrite
*October 19, 2006*

Primo Levi, the Italian writer who gave us probably the most compelling account of life and death in a German concentration camp, told of a recurring nightmare common among inmates. He and his fellow sufferers at Auschwitz dreamt of a time in the future when they were free and were trying to tell people of the horrors in the camps, of the depths of depravity to which human beings are capable of sinking. Despite their desperate efforts to be heard, no one would listen or believe. They cried out and people turned their backs. And this is indeed what happened to Levi himself. For over 10 years, publisher after publisher rejected If This Is a Man, his memoir of Auschwitz. It is now of course an undisputed classic of 20th century literature.

Last Tuesday, a remarkable book was launched in this country. As a manuscript, it lay undiscovered for almost half a century. Its author, Peter Tyrrell, had tragically committed suicide almost 40 years ago by setting himself alight on London's Hampstead Heath. Like Primo Levi, he was determined that people hear his tale of horror, and, like Levi, he was ignored and dismissed. Tyrrell is a rare phenomenon of post-Independence Ireland - he is a genuine hero. His memoir, Founded on Fear, was discovered recently by historian Diarmuid Whelan in the National Library among the papers of the late Senator Owen Sheehy-Skeffington. It tells of the grinding poverty of his childhood in County Galway, and his removal at the age of eight to the industrial school at Letterfrack in Connemara. It also covers his subsequent years in the British army during the Second World War He was wounded and captured in 1945, and memorably describes his German prisoner-of-war camp as "heaven on earth" compared to Letterfrack.

Tyrrell's account of the seven years of his childhood spent at the Christian Brothers' institution has a childlike directness, an absence of self-pity and a unique even-handedness which place his memoir among the most powerful of the genre. Written in 1958, it is also the very earliest such account that we know of, and consequently a document of enormous historical significance. In a powerfully dispassionate manner, largely unburdened by any tone of moralising, he describes the appalling reality of life for a child at Letterfrack during the 1920s and 1930s. He tells of the savage and sadistic beatings administered by a number of Brothers - boys of all ages were usually attacked from behind, so they never knew when it was coming. They were hit repeatedly, often up to 20 times, on the head and back at full force with a variety of weapons, from hefty sticks and leathers to thick rubber strips reinforced with metal wire. Tyrrell recounts the systematic destruction of little boys, his mates, as they are literally in some cases driven mad by the endless torture they experience. On one occasion, his own arm was broken during an attack and he was ordered to tell the doctor that he had fallen down the stairs. Founded on Fear is also a rich and detailed account of daily life in Letterfrack, with all its incomprehensible contradictions. Tyrrell talks about how the Brothers completely changed personality on Christmas Day, playing and joking with the boys in the friendliest fashion. He describes outings arranged by Brothers who went to great lengths to ensure that the children enjoyed themselves. He also refers to Brothers who did not beat the children - by no means all were cruel and vicious. In short, he does not shy away from the oddly schizophrenic nature of these places.

It is this fair-mindedness which has been highlighted by the Christian Brothers in their statement about Tyrrell's book this week. In an unusual step, they have commented favourably on the memoir, and have taken the opportunity both to apologise unreservedly to victims of similar abuse and to acknowledge publicly their failings when during the 1950s Tyrrell himself came to confront them with their abuse of children. It was an extraordinarily brave action on his part. He was concerned that children might be still suffering from such cruelty at their institutions and he wanted it stopped. The Brothers, however, refused to listen. Documents supplied to the Child Abuse Commission show that their primary concern was that he might try to blackmail them. Today, many of those abused at Christian Brother institutions during the very years when Peter Tyrrell was seeking to expose it have been deeply hurt by what they perceive as the Brothers' continuing denial of their responsibility for such widespread crimes against children. In this context, it is important to acknowledge the honesty of the Christian Brothers' statement accepting the validity of Peter Tyrrell's memoir. It is their most generous public utterance to date. It is all that he asked for when he was alive. Even now, so many years after his despairing suicide, it is still not too late to express such sincere contrition.

# Ahern misled the Dáil

*October 26, 2006*

Last Tuesday, the Taoiseach misled the Dáil. The subject was the alleged waste of over half a billion euro of taxpayers' money. This is the additional cost to the State of shouldering the vast bulk of the bill (now up to €1.3 billion) to compensate victims of institutional child abuse.

There has been so much argument about the notorious Church/State deal on redress, which capped the contribution by religious orders at €128 million (less than 10 per cent of the total), that sight has been lost of the major issue. It is not, as the Taoiseach sought to argue this week, about whether some people feel that victims should not be compensated. There is unanimity, both within the Oireachtas and throughout the general population, that financial redress is entirely appropriate. Nor is the issue about whether too much is being paid out to victims, or that people may be applying for compensation who are not entitled to it. (The average payout is, if anything, too low compared to equivalent High Court awards, and there has been no evidence of claimant fraud.) What this is about is the cost of an indemnity. How much is it worth to have the State bail you out if you are sued, covering your legal costs and all awards made against you? When you know, as the religious orders did, that you could be facing tens of thousands of claims, such an indemnity was devoutly to be desired. Getting it so cheaply was like manna from heaven.

The Government has spent years scrabbling about trying to defend what in reality is its (or rather the taxpayers') extraordinary generosity to 18 religious congregations who ran institutions in which children suffered unspeakable abuse. Bertie Ahern was at it again on Tuesday. They couldn't afford to pay anything more than €128 million, he said. However, there is no basis for this. The Comptroller and Auditor General has made clear in his reports that no one from the State ever even asked for information on the assets of the religious orders. Mr Ahern also said that "it was not known how many people were in our institutions that were under State control". Again, not true. The State has always had detailed records of numbers in industrial schools and other institutions, as it paid a fee in respect of each such child. To estimate how many are alive today, it is reasonable to calculate the figures since 1930, as the C&AG has done. This reveals that we are concerned with about 30,000 individuals who grew up in institutional care, and may be eligible for compensation. In fact, less than half have applied - the total now stands at 14,541. The Taoiseach added that the original estimate of cost by the Department of Education was €610 million. This also is untrue. The earliest estimate, communicated by the State to the religious orders, was in fact €254 million, which we now know was a wild miscalculation. However, the final contribution by the orders to the redress scheme ended up at almost exactly 50 per cent of this original estimate, reflecting the State's view at the time that both it and the religious orders were jointly liable for the abuse suffered by children. This joint liability line was repeated in the Dáil by the Taoiseach on Tuesday. "If it had been fought in court, the State would have been jointly liable," he said. (If this is indeed his view, then surely it follows that State and Church should equally share the cost of redress.) However, in 2003 a High Court ruling cast serious doubt over the joint liability argument. In this case, the State was held to have zero liability for the abuse of a child at an institution, and the religious order concerned was judged to be 100 per cent responsible. The basis for this ruling was the manner in which the State conducted the business of industrial schools. It paid the bills, but it left the management of the institutions entirely to the religious orders. Consequently, according to Justice O'Higgins, the State was not liable in the case before him.

In the light of this judgment, which the State has now successfully used as a precedent to argue that it has no liability for child abuse in other, day-school cases, it is difficult to see how the Taoiseach can claim, as he did on Tuesday, that "the State's deeper pockets would have ended up paying the full bill. That is what would have happened legally." Or even his statement that "the State was responsible for these institutions". The truth is that the Government has acted brazenly to protect the assets of the Catholic Church. In doing so, it has exposed the taxpayer to a massive bill for which it transpires the State may have no legal liability. Meanwhile, it continues vindictively to pursue victims of abuse at day-schools, like Louise O'Keeffe, for the enormous legal costs arising from their failed attempts to make the State take responsibility for what happened to them. It would be hard to find a more blatant double standard.

# Health service still in denial
*November 2, 2006*

It has been a grim time for the health service over the past few weeks. It seems that there has been one case after another of people either dying or seriously injured as a direct result of medical treatment.

Minister for Health Mary Harney yesterday expressed concern in this newspaper for patient safety in small regional hospitals. However, the extent of medical error in all hospitals, whether big or small, continues to be overlooked. Last week we heard about Elizabeth O'Mullane, who was told she had breast cancer and subsequently had a partial mastectomy. It later transpired that she didn't have cancer at all. Thus, the operation removing part of her breast was unnecessary and she may be left with long-term health problems as a result. Then there was Alan O'Gorman, the young Dublin man whose stomach was removed after a diagnosis of cancer. All Alan had was an ulcer. His test results had been mixed up with those of an elderly man who did have cancer.

I first met Alan over three years ago, when he told us his story for a Prime Time Investigates programme on medical error. It was not easy for a 20-year-old (as he was then) to go on national television and discuss personal medical details. Alan, however, displayed a determination to ensure that no one else should have to go through the appalling trauma he had suffered. He also decided to take a court case to force someone to take responsibility for his injury. Alan's case eventually came to court last month. The facts were not disputed, and he is to receive compensation for the severe medical consequences he will have to deal with for the rest of his life. However, what was most striking was that no one involved in Alan's treatment was prepared to admit liability or take responsibility for the mistake. As a result, Alan has had to go through years of uncertainty as he waited for his case to be resolved.

Michelle Tallon's parents may be facing similar difficulties. Bernie and Bernard Tallon have spent the past year looking for answers as to why their daughter died at the age of 38 in the James Connolly Memorial Hospital in Blanchardstown. Michelle had cerebral palsy and was unable to speak. She had been cared for all her life by her parents, who were her voice. Admitted to hospital in the summer of 2005 with suspected gastroenteritis, she went steadily downhill, according to her parents. She died two weeks later. Last month, the jury at her inquest recorded a verdict of medical misadventure. What this somewhat archaic term means is that Michelle's death was the direct result of the medical treatment she received at the hospital. However, the verdict does not provide any further detail, and for Michelle's parents major questions remain. They had serious complaints with the way their daughter was cared for by the hospital. They hardly left Michelle's bedside during her stay. They repeatedly asked to see the doctors in charge of their daughter. It took a week before they were seen. They constantly questioned the presence of the nil per oral (NPO) order above Michelle's bed, meaning that she should not be fed. They were becoming increasingly alarmed by Michelle's weakened state. The hospital conducted a risk management report into Michelle's death. Risk management is one of those new processes designed to reassure us that hospitals and medics will be fully open when things go wrong and that mistakes will be learnt from. The report on Michelle deals with the NPO order. It concludes that the absence of "a specific policy relating to the day-to-day management of a 'nil-by-mouth' order . . . may have led to the possibility of an order remaining in force for longer than it was intended, either through miscommunication or misunderstanding between medical and nursing staff". The report does not indicate whether this may have been a factor in her death, which was caused by acute respiratory distress syndrome. Given that the NPO order was such a key concern of Michelle's parents, the vagueness of the language in the risk management report, the use of words like "may" and "possibility", does not answer their very legitimate concerns that their daughter was not properly fed in hospital. There are also a number of confusing discrepancies between the contents of the risk-management report and some of the evidence presented at Michelle's inquest. All of this means that her parents remain in the dark as to what exactly caused Michelle's death.

And lest anyone think that what happened to Michelle, or to Alan O'Gorman or Elizabeth O'Mullane is a rare or unusual event, it is worth recalling the view of the Department of Health on the extent of medical error in this country. In 2001, it acknowledged that up to six patients each day die in Irish hospitals as a direct result of preventable medical error. Those brave few prepared to battle for answers deserve more from a system still all too willing to bury its mistakes.

# Tactics of Mater are disturbing
*November 9, 2006*

There are a handful of events that have the capacity to reduce one to almost incoherent outrage. One of these occurred in early October, although we only heard about it this week. It is the hounding and bullying by the Mater hospital of former cancer patient Janette Byrne.

Janette is one of those rare individuals who is prepared to stand up and be counted, even when literally flat on her back on a hospital bed (or even a trolley). She has been one of the leading voices for patients suffering the callous indignities of a chaotic health service over the past four years. Through Patients Together, the campaigning group she founded, and in her recent book, If It Were Only Cancer , she has displayed a thoroughly laudable determination to fight for the rights of all current and future patients within the system. The Mater hospital has taken grave exception to her book. However, rather than the more usual course of perhaps issuing a public statement expressing disagreement with Janette's views, the hospital has instead chosen a different and considerably more threatening option. It instructed its solicitors to write to the book's publishers, Veritas. They stated that Janette had defamed the hospital, that she had attacked staff without giving them a right to reply and that her book contained factual misstatements and exaggerations.

What is remarkable about this is that Janette was at some pains in her book to commend the commitment, care and general good humour of many of the staff members she came across, singling out a number of doctors and nurses for special praise. What she describes in sometimes gruesome detail and with searing honesty is how it feels to be weak, sick and helpless within a system that is profoundly dysfunctional. It is clear that the Mater's response is an example of that dysfunction - if anything, Janette's book and campaign should be welcomed by an institution dedicated to the care of sick people. Instead, the hospital seeks to silence Janette. It has provided not a shred of evidence that anything in her book is inaccurate. Its defensiveness and bullying tactics are deeply disturbing in an organisation that has been chosen to have a leading role in the new national children's hospital, now to be located on the Mater complex.

In this context, it is worth looking at who exactly controls the Mater hospital and who is likely to have taken the decision to try and silence Janette Byrne. (Their PR company, Slattery Communications, refused to tell me which boards or bodies within the Mater had discussed the issue of her book.) The ownership of the Mater's parent company resides with the Sisters of Mercy, who make up a majority of the shareholders, or more accurately the company members. For the record (and because they are not named anywhere on the Mater's website), they are: Sr Helena O'Donoghue (one of the negotiators of the infamous Church/State deal on redress for institutional child abuse), Sr Helen Keegan, Sr Cait O'Dwyer, Sr Esther Murphy, Sr Geraldine Collins and Sr Fionnula Glynn. The members of the hospital's board of governors do appear on the website (www.mater.ic). They comprise Cardinal Desmond Connell and a number of academics, medics, businessmen and a judge. There is also one priest, Fr Kevin Doran (described as an ethicist), and two Sisters of Mercy.

The chair of the board is businessman Desmond Lamont. Last September, he sparked a major row with the Health Service Executive by stating the hope that the 150th anniversary of the Mater would be marked by the opening of the new national children's hospital on the complex. Describing Mr Lamont's remarks as "disingenuous, presumptuous and unhelpful in the extreme", head of the HSE Brendan Drumm said the decision as to when it would open would not be taken by the Mater. Prof Drumm also indicated that the new children's facility would be independently governed. However, it has not been explained exactly how this independence will be achieved.

Given what we now know about the Mater's attitude to patients such as Janette Byrne who fearlessly speak out about the inadequacies of the service provided, it is a matter of urgency for the HSE to clarify the precise nature of the future connections between the new children's hospital and the Mater. This is all the more important in the light of what we discovered last year about the Mater's attitude to cancer research. The hospital's clinical trials advisory group decided the use of certain experimental drugs carrying a warning against pregnancy for those taking them was contrary to its Catholic ethos, as it might encourage the use of artificial contraception. In the face of a public furore, the hospital board was forced to reverse the decision. It should be remembered that despite its entirely private ownership, the Mater hospital receives public funding of over €200 million a year. It consequently should be accountable to us, the taxpayers, for all its actions and policies, including the disgraceful attempts to silence Janette Byrne.

# Boot camp plan merits the boot

*November 23, 2006*

It is all too easy to dismiss Fine Gael's latest idea of Army-run boot camps for young offenders as a mad-cap scheme, in the words of Minister for Justice Michael McDowell this week. This is not to say that they are a good idea - far from it. But the Minister's reaction does contain a rich element of the kettle calling the pot black.

But to deal firstly with Fine Gael. The boot camp notion has come from Billy Timmins TD, the party's spokesman on defence, and a former Army officer. He clearly has such a high opinion of his previous employer's capabilities that he thinks they can sort out the highly complex problem of juvenile delinquency without even the slightest training in the area. If it was just Billy Timmins's idea, though, one might not be too worried. However, he has been quoted as saying that it was his party leader, Enda Kenny, who asked him to examine the proposal. If this indicates the extent of Fine Gael's thinking on youth justice, then it represents an appalling level of ignorance. Internationally, the militaristic approach to young offenders, the short sharp shock treatment, has been shown to be both highly ineffectual and savagely abusive. Some of the stories emerging from these kinds of institutions elsewhere are genuinely hair-raising, to the extent that they are increasingly being either shut down or severely controlled.

Primarily designed to break children, they typically employ the drill sergeant tactic of intimidation by yelling in their faces and punishing physical chores and exercises. One can hear the baying from a chorus of Fine Gael TDs already - good enough for them, the hooded thugs who make life a misery for hard-working, law-abiding citizens. Vote for us and we'll hand them over to the Army to give them a taste of their own medicine. It is hard to think of a more unsuitable agency than the military for dealing with children. An army is premised on the legitimate use of force (or violence) to pursue the aims of the state, both internally and externally, and to which end its members are trained to kill. It embodies the ultimate in authoritarianism, demanding unquestioning obedience to orders. (This is not particularly unreasonable in the context of its purpose - concepts of consensus and widespread consultation are hardly feasible on the battlefield.)

In Ireland, though, we have a tendency to think of the Army as a kind of super-aid agency, going out into the world to do good deeds and keep the peace. While not without an element of truth, this perception is largely misguided. The Army itself views peace-keeping as an opportunity to provide it with vital operational experience. If a military force does not know how to fight, has had no experience of danger and battle, one could certainly validly question if it has any function at all. While the nation can justifiably take considerable pride in the acclaimed professionalism of Irish soldiers in their peace-keeping activities, to confuse this with the idea that the Army is a suitable body to deal with troubled or criminal youth is dangerous nonsense. In case Fine Gael has forgotten, we used to hand children (most of them not criminal at all) over to untrained people who ran the precursors of the kind of boot camps proposed. These of course were the industrial schools, and we are all too familiar with their legacy of terror and abuse. It is truly staggering that this party could propose a measure which would negate overnight the painstaking lessons which society is slowly learning from its mistakes.

However, while Fianna Fáil and the PDs gleefully pour scorn on the boot camp notion, their own record in Government in terms of the treatment of juvenile offenders is hardly without blemish. They preside over a regime for the detention of young people for which the inspector of prisons, Mr Justice Dermot Kinlen, has said they should be ashamed of themselves. He has demanded that St Patrick's Institution for young offenders should be immediately destroyed. Despite this, it appears that it will remain with us until at least 2011. In addition, the sections of the Children's Act 2001 dealing with the appointment of an inspector for children's detention schools were never enacted. Consequently, no such inspector has been appointed. Even worse, new legislation is now in place which substantially waters down the provisions for independent inspection of such schools. Furthermore, the Children's Ombudsman remains excluded from the area.

It would be foolish to minimise the problem of anti-social behaviour by youngsters in certain areas. It is also true that detention quite properly continues to be a sanction for youngsters who break the law. However, there is a growing awareness that it is useful only as a last resort. A range of earlier interventions by highly trained professionals are now viewed as being far more likely to effect behavioural change. It is the heavy resourcing of these policies which will assist the children themselves to control their own behaviour.

# Conning the elderly yet again
*December 14, 2006*

You have to hand it to the Government. They are nothing if not ingenious. Their latest wheeze is stunning - run a system into the ground so badly that it becomes indefensible, and then use its faults to justify making people pay through the nose for it. The proposed new scheme to charge for nursing home care brilliantly taps into the Irish zeitgeist of spend now and pay later. There is no more talk of people's rights.

The devilish cunning of it in this case is that payback happens only when you are dead. The one simple message that Minister for Health Mary Harney has been hammering home all week is that most of us do not realise just how bad things are at the moment. Elderly people are forced to sell their homes, or to get in hock to the banks, or their children are reduced to penury - all to pay for current nursing home care. Very true. But who, one might reasonably ask, is responsible for such reprehensible and heartless hounding of the aged, the infirm and their offspring? Surely not the very same people who now so roundly condemn their own system? It is worth delving back into the mists of time - well, the last general election in fact - to recall a solemn promise made by the current Government. It was the guarantee of a medical card, and consequently free medical treatment, to everyone over 70. The cynical among us categorised it as an attempt, stunningly successful as it turned out, to buy the election. The rest of us, however, thought that it was an excellent scheme, and we happily bought into the rhetoric of Government ministers who said it was time to give something back from the Celtic Tiger to those whose sacrifices in leaner times had paved the way for our current bonanza.

In our naivety, we all thought that free medical care for the over-70s included being treated when they were too sick to look after themselves. This time last year, when it emerged that elderly patients' pensions were being illegally taken away from them to fund nursing home care, we realised that we had been conned. While the Government was forced to repay these ill-gotten gains, it also moved with unseemly haste to make the pension deductions fully legal from that point on. This had previously been regarded as so politically risky a proposal that for decades no one had had the nerve to confront the secretive and illegal deductions scheme. It was noteworthy that, in the midst of the maelstrom of criticism surrounding the stolen pensions, there were no serious objections to the principle of making all elderly people pay towards their full-time care. The flights of fancy before the previous general election about older people entitled as of right to medical care were jettisoned overnight, and the public barely seemed to notice. It was a lesson not lost on Government. Having established the principle that elderly people should pay, it has now upped the ante and moved to the next stage by giving itself the right to get its hands on people's assets, namely their homes.

The spectre has been raised that with an ageing population, the cost to the State of caring for older people will become astronomical, and thus unsustainable in the long term. However, geriatricians will tell you that on the contrary, as medical advances mean healthier old people, the proportion in need of full-time care will not increase substantially. Despite changes in Irish society, that percentage has remained remarkably stable. In the late 1960s, for instance, roughly 5 per cent of those over 65 were in long-stay care. Today, it is 4.6 per cent. There has, however, been one significant shift. In the 1960s, four out of every five beds for long-stay elderly care were in the public sector. Now, over half of the beds are provided by private interests, whose primary motivation is profit. Remarkable, is it not, that during a period four decades ago when the country was so impoverished, we managed through State care to look after most of those elderly people in need, without making them give up part of their houses? It is profoundly disturbing how little public discussion there has been on this issue. The Government lists numerous reports on the care of the elderly, but this hardly qualifies as debate, particularly as none of them involved widespread public consultation with the stakeholders involved. Their conclusions on how to fund nursing home care varied widely. The Mercer Report in 2002, for instance, strongly favoured a social insurance scheme, a kind of extension of PRSI, with care available without additional charge to everyone who needed it. Interestingly, this report ruled out the idea of a tax on people's estates (which is effectively what has now been introduced). An estate tax, it stated, "would not garner sufficient public or political acceptance to be a viable policy option". Mary Harney cannot say she wasn't warned.

# Fatima's little miracles
*December 28, 2006*

Children and concepts of childhood have received unusual prominence in the news during the past year. From statutory rape to the age of consent, issues relating to young people have been endlessly discussed. In some cases, children have even been asked what they think. The questions, however, are phrased by adults. They deal primarily with our concerns rather than with theirs.

Children almost never get the opportunity to create their own agendas, to bring what is important to them into the public domain. While adults have created for them groupings such as Dáil na nÓg or mini-United Nations, these simply replicate grown-up structures. The true voices and stories of children are much harder to find. And when we do get to hear them, what they tell us is often surprising. On the Block is a half-hour documentary made entirely by the children of Dublin's Fatima Mansions. It was shown on RTÉ on Christmas Day and was the culmination of two years of filming by the children, all of whom were under the age of 12.

Fatima Mansions, with its 14 blocks of Dublin City Council flats, has frequently been interpreted to us by outsiders. Film crews and journalists descend periodically on the area to explain to us how awful it is, with its drugs and its crime and its hopelessness.
It is an image against which many of the local people have railed. Certainly there were severe problems, but why define an entire community exclusively in negative terms, they asked. They were upset, for instance, by the remarks of High Court judge Paul Carney during a manslaughter trial last year. He had spoken of being haunted by descriptions of conditions "at the cruelly named Fatima Mansions". The court heard during the trial that "people were told 'go left for the white stuff and go right for the brown stuff' when looking for drugs at the block of flats". Justice Carney specifically referred to the large number of young people who had died before being able to give evidence at the trial.

This was certainly part of the truth about Fatima. But alongside it was the reality of hundreds of families getting on with their lives in the flats while combining together to form what has become one of the strongest and most vibrant community groupings in the country. They have involved themselves at every stage of the regeneration of their area, a €200 million project which is now well under way. The old 1950s blocks are being demolished to make way for new houses

127

and apartments, a mixture of public and private housing. The opening of the first phase of the redevelopment in 2005 was featured in the children's documentary on their lives in the flats. Crowds of dignitaries were there for what was a good-news story. Bertie Ahern was seen on the evening news cutting the red ribbon on the spanking new houses for the local residents. In a well-publicised moment at the time, 11-year-old Sean Mulvaney was seen squaring up to the Taoiseach to ask him when the children would get proper play facilities. The answer was unclear and the cameras moved on.

In On The Block, however, we saw the episode from a different and novel perspective - that of the children themselves. One of them managed to get a camera up close to Bertie as Sean Mulvaney questioned him. We perceived the Taoiseach from a child's view, a much lower angle than usual. We also saw more than was on the news. As Sean pursued him on the issue of play facilities, the smile on Bertie's face became strained as he changed the subject rapidly. "So listen, it's good to see you anyway," said the Taoiseach as he moved off. While the children clearly delighted in questioning the various politicians who arrived from time to time in the flats, their film is much more about the ordinary business of being a child. Their focus in on their games, their friends and how they spend their time, rather than on social problems or community agitation. They do mention the drugs, the drinking, the shouting and the crime, and how they would change all that if they had a magic wand. But it does not consume them or get them down. They talk about looking forward to having new houses, but also their sadness at losing the flats. We see some of them keeping bits of their old wallpaper to remind them of their homes. What they show us through On The Block is that children are children regardless of the environments in which they live. They have the same vitality, energy, joy and mischief as any other children in the country. A statement of the obvious, perhaps, but one which bears repeating in the context of our continuing tendency to blacken and sensationalise particular areas and estates on the basis of their deprivation status or crime statistics. And by the way, the children of Fatima Mansions still have not been provided with decent play facilities.

# Hail those ludicrous anthems
*February 22, 2007*

At the heart of much of the pomposity surrounding the Croke Park anthems debate lies an overwhelming silliness. Grown men - and it does seem to be mainly men involved - are becoming greatly exercised over the singing of a collection of anachronistic lines in songs whose meaning has become so obscure and hackneyed as to be rendered nonsensical.

Leaving aside for the moment the bizarre reality that few of us in this country can even understand our own anthem, a reading of the English translation - available on the website of the Department of the Taoiseach - displays it in all its foolishness. All one can do is laugh helplessly at its exhortation to the "Sons of the Gael! Men of the Pale" to "set the Tyrant quaking". Aside from being a ludicrous notion in this day and age, it baldly excludes the half of the population who are neither sons nor men. Further, the idea of a neutral country with an anthem entitled The Soldier's Song is nearly as farcical as that of a long-established democracy whose national hymn focuses so intently on the saving of its monarch.

For every accusation of belligerence and bellicosity hurled at God Save the Queen, there is an equal or even more savage one that can be applied to ourselves. While the British have had the good manners to largely drop their verse which relishes the oppression of Scotland ("And like a torrent rush, rebellious Scots to crush"), we in this country persist somewhat pathetically in clinging to our lines about "the Saxon foe". It would be churlish to deny that lifting the myopic ban on foreign games in Croke Park is anything but a welcome mark of progress, particularly as it was done by the GAA in the full knowledge that foreign anthems would sully that hallowed ground. However, arguably as great a leap forward was the gesture by the IRFU to sacrifice Amhrán na bhFiann entirely at rugby matches played away from home out of sensitivity to the Northern Irish members of the squad. Its replacement, Ireland's Call, has at least the virtue of being relatively inoffensive. Which cannot be said for a number of the anthems we may now hear at Croke Park.

Take the French, for instance. La Marseillaise, that great, rousing rally cry against oppression, exults ghoulishly in the prospect of watering French fields with impure blood - a fond desire to exsanguinate foreigners rather than a reference to recent transfusion scandals (of which France has had its share). It is hardly a helpful sentiment in the face of France's troubled multiethnic identity.

And spare a thought for the poor Germans, who have spent decades trying to live down the wildly supremacist overtones of their anthem. Jubilantly belted out by the Nazis, the first verse - the Deutschland Uber Alles one, translated as

"Germany over all, over everything in the world" - has been officially excised from the anthem for over 60 years. But it is still what everyone, German or not, has in their heads when the tune strikes up. On official occasions, however, only the third verse is sung. It is harmless enough, full of blooming happiness and brotherhood. Sisters get a look-in, but only in the second stanza, which lists - in the following order - German women, German loyalty, German wine and German song as inspirations for noble deeds.

This kind of nonsense is depressingly typical of national anthems in general, a form of expression in which people seem to lose all sense of judgment, taste, discernment and even common sense. There has been the odd attempt in recent years to change the offensively sexist nature of some of them. In Austria, for instance, objections were raised to the exclusively male references, including the line "you are home to great sons", and the usual homage to fatherland and brotherhood. They got nowhere, however, and the paradigm of the heroic male and the decorative female adjunct - if the latter is mentioned at all - remains paramount, particularly in Western anthems.

Undoubtedly among the more entertaining, though, is Slovenia's national song. It is an ode to wine, taken to such an extreme that each verse on the page forms the shape of a wine glass. While it also touches all the tiresome bases - the brotherhood of men, the beauty of the maidens and cheerful slaughter of all enemies - the emphasis on alcohol, "to summon hope out of despair", is refreshing. Sadly, however, only one verse, predictably the most banal, constitutes the official anthem.

Finally, a modest suggestion for next Saturday at Croke Park. In the plethora of anthems and national songs to be sung, could we not add one more - just a little one, which could do us the great service of placing all others in the context they so richly deserve? It goes something like this:
"Hail, Hail Freedonia,
Mightiest of mighty nations.
Hail, hail Freedonia,
Land of the brave and free."

# Price for doing State a service

*March 15, 2007*

You take your life in your hands these days if you happen to be asked by the State to inquire into a matter of major public concern. Prof Des O'Neill, who produced the report on the Leas Cross nursing home, found out the hard way that doing the State some service is a risky business. There are circumstances where there is a clear necessity for a full statutory tribunal or commission of inquiry, complete with all the cumbersome legal paraphernalia. However, there are other cases, such as Leas Cross, where a more limited but considerably faster inquiry process may be preferable. Those asked to perform the latter task are carefully selected. Their specific expertise and their independence are critical determinants. They are the kind of people the public will both believe and trust. Their verdicts are consequently enormously influential in shaping both public opinion and government policy in the wake of allegations of injustice, wrongdoing or incompetence. Given that it is the State which invariably appoints such individuals, and that most subjects of inquiry concern State business in some shape or form, it is clear that there should never be even the slightest suspicion that the State or its agents have sought to influence the outcome of any inquiry.

Prof O'Neill, a consultant geriatrician, had been asked to examine the records of residents at Leas Cross in response to the enormous public concern provoked by the RTÉ Prime Time documentary on the nursing home. Last May, he delivered his report to the Health Service Executive (HSE), with its now well-known conclusion that conditions at Leas Cross amounted to institutional abuse of the elderly residents. He was also highly critical of the HSE for its lack of proper monitoring of the home. It should be remembered that it was the HSE itself which had commissioned his investigation. For almost six months, the HSE sat on his report. It cited legal difficulties as the reason for the delay in publication. We now know that what in fact was happening was that the HSE was pressurising Prof O'Neill to revise the entire report by including the responses of those criticised within it. Prof O'Neill refused to do so, saying that this could involve quasi-judicial oral hearings, with all sides legally represented, in other words a full-blown tribunal, and was in any event outside his terms of reference. It was at this point that he received a letter from the HSE which can be reasonably construed as containing a threat of the most serious nature. The letter stated that "the indemnity which you consider you have from the HSE may not apply".

For anyone investigating and reporting on major public scandals, an indemnity is clearly vital. It means that the State will protect them in the event that anyone who they determine responsible for wrongdoing or incompetence might sue for defamation. Without such an indemnity, those who agree to take on the responsibility of investigating issues of public concern simply cannot function. The possibility that they could be sued in their private capacity for their public findings would make it impossible for them to report the truth without fear or favour. What is particularly disturbing is that this is not the first time the State has threatened to withdraw indemnity from an investigating group.

Madonna House was the largest residential childcare home in the State during 1980s and into the 1990s. When it emerged that a number of children had been sexually abused there over a long period, the government responded by appointing an inquiry team. Its report was published in 1996, but with the striking omission of almost all the sections dealing directly with who knew what about the abuse, when they knew and what they did about it. The official reason for the complete excision of entire chapters was that it was done "on legal advice". The members of the inquiry team were told by the State that if any part of the banned sections was leaked publicly, their indemnities would be immediately withdrawn from them, and they would become personally liable should anyone sue. This threat was so effective that the truth of what happened in Madonna House remained secret for years.

The use of the indemnity threat seriously questions the integrity of all future non-statutory inquiries and reviews of the Leas Cross kind. While Prof O'Neill refused to back down, he has himself said that he felt he was "in an exceptionally exposed position". Although the HSE did eventually withdraw its letter raising questions about Prof O'Neill's indemnity, the whole affair has fatally undermined the State's credibility in assuring us that independent inquiries can and will expose the whole truth of any scandal, past, present or future.

# Women victims seek truth

*March 22, 2007*

It has been described in unforgettable terms as a barbaric procedure which opened up a woman like a hinge during childbirth. "Midwifery of darker times," was the view of one leading British obstetrician. However, far from being a Dark Ages practice, it was performed frequently in some of this country's leading maternity hospitals until the 1980s. Symphysiotomy, as it is called, consists of permanently widening a woman's pelvis during childbirth by slicing through the cartilage joining the pubic bones. The Human Rights Commission has now begun a preliminary investigation of the practice with a view to establishing whether it fits its criteria for a full inquiry. So far, the efforts of the survivors of the procedure to get at the truth of what happened to them have been largely ignored by the State.

Hundreds of Irish women were operated on in this way from the 1940s. About 200 remain alive today, and life-long side effects include difficulty in walking, severe back pain and persistent incontinence. Most were not told of the procedure at the time of their operations, and never knew the reasons for their chronic health problems. It is clear that the practice had been internationally discredited long before it was discarded in this country, and fundamental questions remain as to why women were made to suffer so unnecessarily in this way. After questions were raised in the Dáil in 2003, the Government promised an investigation by an independent expert. This never materialised, and remains a broken promise. The huge concern surrounding the symphysiotomy procedure is that it may have been carried out primarily for religious rather than medical reasons. A number of prominent obstetricians had lauded the procedure during the 1950s as an alternative to Caesarean section, not because the latter was unsafe, but because the risks associated with future deliveries after a Caesarean might lead women to use artificial contraception, which was of course contrary to Catholic teaching.

The group of women concerned were dealt a serious blow last year when the High Court dismissed the case of Olivia Kearney. Hers was the first symphysiotomy action to come before the courts. In 1969, at the age of 18, her baby was born by Caesarean section at the Lourdes hospital in Drogheda. Her obstetrician, Dr Gerard Connolly, then carried out a symphysiotomy on her. According to evidence presented by both herself and her GP, neither was informed that she had undergone this procedure. She only discovered it when she sought and obtained her medical records from the hospital in 2002. Dr Connolly, as head of the maternity unit at the Lourdes hospital, had presided over a total of 348 symphysiotomies at the hospital between the early 1950s and 1982, when he retired and the practice terminated abruptly. He had been employed at the hospital as an obstetrician a bare five years after graduation, and without any of the usual post-graduate obstetric qualifications. He was described as a deeply religious man, "revered" by the nuns who ran the hospital. He maintained the practice of symphysiotomy for decades after even the main Dublin Catholic maternity hospitals had abandoned it. Ms Kearney had sued the Medical Missionaries of Mary, who owned the hospital until 1997. They sought to have her action struck out on the basis that there was an inexcusable delay in bringing it before the courts, which was such as to severely prejudice their right to a fair hearing. Ms Justice Anne Dunne ruled in their favour and against Ms Kearney. During the hearing, the nuns had denied everything, even that a symphysiotomy had taken place. Ms Justice Dunne, however, found to the contrary. She further stated that "it would be no exaggeration to say that she [Olivia Kearney] has been left with a legacy of problems including pain, which could not but have had a significant adverse effect on many aspects of her life." The judge also expressed "the utmost sympathy for the plight in which she now finds herself." Nonetheless, given that Dr Connolly was deceased, as were many of the other staff members involved in Olivia Kearney's care, the judge ruled that it would be unjust to ask the nuns to defend themselves in court. She consequently dismissed the case against them.

The issue of how to deal with people injured as a result of actions which took place in the past remains a difficult one. The judgment above is very in keeping with the courts' view that distance of time can prejudice a fair hearing. A number of cases, including some against disgraced obstetrician Michael Neary, were thrown out on similar grounds. It is now clear that a political rather than a legal solution should be found in these cases. It is right and proper that the Government acknowledged the damage done to the victims of Michael Neary by establishing both a full inquiry and a compensation scheme. The victims of symphysiotomy deserve no less.

# State's indifference to victims
*March 29, 2007*

There is something particularly unedifying about the spectacle of a Government Minister slithering away from responsibility. When that responsibility involves the duty of the State to ensure the safety of children, it is especially reprehensible.

Minister for Education Mary Hanafin attempted last week to defend the legal tactics of the State, which has recently threatened hundreds of victims of child sexual abuse in national schools that if they did not immediately drop their cases against her department, they would be actively pursued for enormous legal costs. It was all the lawyers, she said in an interview on RTÉ news. She claimed to know nothing about the threatening letters, nor did she sanction them. "It was very much a legal letter going to other lawyers. It wasn't in any way intended to upset or to offend ... It was never sent to the clients themselves," she said. What a relief! It will be a great comfort to victims of abuse that all this business about them having to pay huge costs was merely a housekeeping matter between lawyers, "a legal response to a legal question", according to the Minister in charge.

It is difficult to know what kind of a world Mary Hanafin inhabits. It must be a happy clappy sort of a place, where no one need bother their fluffy little heads about lawyers or letters or costs or anything nasty like that. To most people, who incidentally have a somewhat firmer grasp on reality, notification from the State (whether sent to them or their lawyers) of a determination to come after them for hundreds of thousands of euro in legal costs is a terrifying threat. It is not the first time a government has engaged in this kind of legal intimidation of victims. Describing similar tactics 10 years ago, the following statements were made in the Dáil: "the government has been involved in covert and ruthless campaigns to frustrate the victims ... Is the minister [ and government colleagues] asking the people of Ireland to accept they were doing their job properly by trying to suggest they were in blissful ignorance of the way the case was being handled?" This was the current Minister for Finance, Brian Cowen, quite properly excoriating the then coalition government for its vindictive handling of the case of Brigid McCole, a victim of Hepatitis C. Its excuse at the time, that its actions were for legal reasons, is strikingly similar to the defence now being trotted out by Mary Hanafin for her treatment of another set of victims of State indifference.

It would be hard to better Brian Cowen's trenchant criticism of a politician who hides behind lawyers in this way. "Such legal fictions will not wash. Political responsibility cannot be abdicated away with fanciful legalisms which portray the political master . . . of this tragic case as if it were somebody else's business. Even the Minister would have to concede that that falls far short of the most minimalist definition of political accountability."

It is interesting in the light of the above to note that Brian Cowen himself may have played a role in the settlement of one of the earlier national school abuse cases against the State. Aiden O'Brien, a constituent of his, appealed to him for assistance when difficulties arose in terms of the State defendants paying out the full amount of damages agreed on in his case. Liability for the sexual abuse suffered by Aiden as a young child had been jointly accepted in 2005 by the State and by the religious order involved in the Co Offaly primary school concerned - in which incidentally Brian Cowen himself had been a pupil around the same time. A dispute then arose between the State and the religious order. Compensation to Aiden and other victims was put on the long finger. Almost immediately after his appeal to Brian Cowen, Aiden received his compensation, paid out in full by the State. This is an example of a government and a minister behaving properly, responsibly and with the kind of humanity one should expect in the context of their historic and clearly sincere apology in 1999 to victims of child abuse.

It is, however, in sharp contrast to what is happening now. During the research for the Prime Time programme which I made on the subject last week, I came across a number of cases of individuals raped and sexually abused as children in national schools who have been forced to abandon their cases against the Department of Education out of fear that they could face bankruptcy - simply for seeking justice and accountability from the State, which, after all, compelled them to go to school in the first place. Others are literally risking everything they have by fighting on. They have been shocked by Ms Hanafin's description of them last week as pursuing their cases for reasons of "retribution". The despair they feel at the Government's refusal to take responsibility for what happened to them in what is officially a "national" school system is something we should all feel ashamed of.

# Consultant greed lies unmasked
*April 19, 2007*

At last we are able to glimpse what lies at the core of negotiations on the new contract for hospital consultants. As the talks waxed and waned with excruciating slowness over the past four years, the ground continually shifted. Every conceivable obstacle has been grasped by consultants to hinder the introduction of a vital reform within the system. One minute it is the issue of clinical indemnity that holds everything up. The next, the problem is supposed interference in the doctor/patient relationship. For the past few months the consultants have been telling us that their main objection to the proposed new contract is that it contains what has been dubbed a gagging clause, curbing their right to advocate on behalf of patients.

This week, however, the smokescreens lifted. The Irish Hospital Consultants' Association deserves credit for the shattering clarity with which it explained its problems. "Mickey Mouse" was the term they used on Tuesday to describe the offer made to them of a new annual salary of €205,000 plus bonuses of €40,000. Faced with such a derisory offer, the IHCA has abandoned negotiations and intends taking industrial action. This salary is designed for public-only consultants. Those wishing to continue supplementing their income with private work will continue to be allowed to do so. The offer to them is a salary of €185,000. This is for a 39-hour week, but 20 per cent of those hours are allowed to be used for private, fee-earning work. The remainder is to be taken up with the treatment of public patients only. In other words, consultants are being offered what by any standards is an enormous salary for a mere 31 hours a week of public hospital work.

"Mickey Mouse" is not how any other consultant in the world working in the public system would describe such an offer. International comparisons (OECD health statistics, 2006) show that Irish consultants earn among the highest salaries anywhere in the developed world. Include their private fees, and Irish earnings become stratospheric. With all the verbiage about advocacy and clinical independence pushed to one side, what we are left with is the obscene spectacle of a group of individuals motivated by naked greed. It is difficult to believe that this motivation applies equally to all consultants. Many share a very real dedication to patients, whether public or private, and a burning desire to see people treated fairly and properly. A number have courageously spoken out, highlighting gross inadequacies within the system. For this group, the so-called gagging clause is a serious problem. However, it does not appear that the HSE actually has any intention of silencing consultants. The relevant clauses in the new contract to be offered to anyone who applies on foot of the advertisements published today for the new consultant posts contain nothing which could remotely be described as a gagging clause. Directly the opposite, in fact. The new contract clearly states that consultants "may advocate on behalf of patients". The only limitations are that they must first raise matters with their line management, and that they should make clear that their public comments are made in a private capacity - hardly unreasonable or draconian conditions, and in fact far more generous than those applying in almost any other kind of employment. Under the heading of "confidentiality" they are required not to divulge any confidential patient or staff information. Again, no evidence here of a conspiracy to silence doctors campaigning for better healthcare.

In the light of this, it seems clear that there is a group of consultants, centred mainly in the IHCA, who are attempting to present themselves as patient champions, facing gagging orders from hospitals and heroically determined not to back down in the face of such bullying tactics. The reality, however, is that they have shamelessly fabricated an issue which does not exist in order to hide the true basis of their opposition to the new contracts - namely the shocking view that a salary of almost a quarter of a million euro is "Mickey Mouse".

The IHCA has already been seriously discredited by its role in the Michael Neary scandal, during which it actively sought to facilitate his remaining in practice after the midwife whistle-blowers had reported his grotesque malpractice to the health board.
Its placement of self-interest at the heart of its activities is most certainly not in the interests of patients. Nor indeed is it ultimately in the interests of doctors or even consultants. As a counter to the IHCA, it is interesting that the Irish Medical Organisation has not walked away from the negotiations on the new consultant contract, nor has it threatened industrial action. The IMO represents a minority of consultants, but the majority of junior hospital doctors. In this context, it has the potential to remain a voice of sanity, allowing us to cling to the notion that there are doctors within the system who are motivated by concerns other than pure greed.

# Cheating abuse victims

*April 26, 2007*

Ron McCartan broke down and cried in Court Number 4 at the Four Courts in Dublin last Tuesday as his family gathered around to comfort him. It had been a seven-year battle, but was a moment he had yearned for almost his entire life. It was also a moment which should have the most profound implications for the largest compensation scheme ever established in this country. Ron is 61 years old. At the age of 10, he was sent to Artane Industrial School, where he was raped repeatedly by one Christian Brother and severely beaten by others. In this regard, as he says himself, he was not unusual. "Many, many other boys suffered the same," he told me yesterday. "We've had to live our whole lives feeling humiliated and worthless because of what they did to us as children." What does make Ron unique, however, is that he decided to fight both the State and the Christian Brothers through the courts, instead of opting for the compensation scheme available through the Residential Institutions Redress Board (RIRB). With the final settlement of his case on Tuesday, Ron received damages of €350,000. This far exceeds anything paid out to date by the RIRB. But what caused Ron to cry was the personal apology to himself from both the Christian Brothers and the State, which was read into the court record. It was the culmination of his absolute determination that they publicly acknowledge the damage they had done to him as a child.

This is not an option for anyone going through the RIRB. For them there is no personal apology, no acceptance of individual responsibility from those who destroyed their childhoods and their lives. All they get is a sum of money, which has now been shown to be substantially less than might be available through the judicial process. Of the almost 15,000 people to apply to the RIRB, roughly 7,000 have now had their cases heard. The average payout is €70,000, less than a quarter of Ron's settlement. Of the larger awards, a minuscule number (well below 1 per cent) have received over €200,000, with only a single individual getting the maximum of €300,000. The overwhelming majority (80 per cent) have received under €100,000. In addition, the average amount awarded has steadily declined since the RIRB began its hearings four years ago. It was always a premise of the scheme, repeated by numerous Government Ministers, that the payments would be at a level commensurate with High Court awards. The problem is that no court has as yet ruled on damages specific to abuse suffered in a residential institution. There is, however, some indication that the RIRB amounts have been well below what the courts might award. In 2003, in what became known as "the visitor case", a man sued both the State and the Irish Sisters of Charity for the sexual abuse he suffered as a child while visiting a friend in the industrial school in Kilkenny. This was a single incident of abuse, perpetrated by a male childcare worker at the institution, and was described by the judge as being at "the lower end of the scale of sexual abuse". However, in recognition of the trauma suffered, he awarded the victim damages of €75,000. There have, in addition, been a number of high-profile cases of individuals sexually abused as children by priests and teachers where the damages awarded by the courts have substantially exceeded the maximum paid out by the RIRB.

It is also increasingly apparent that many of those who have had their cases heard by the board have emerged feeling hurt, humiliated and damaged by the process. They are further subjected to the gag clause in the legislation which makes it a criminal offence for them to reveal how much they received or what happened at the hearings.

"No one can tell me to keep quiet anymore," says Ron. "All our lives, we had this secret, that we'd been abused and tortured. I went to court because I wanted them to apologise directly to me personally, to have to say my name. With the redress board, all you get is a bit of money, usually a pittance, and then you have to keep quiet about it. That's just wrong."

It is difficult to believe that it was the intention of those who established the redress board that victims should feel bullied and humiliated by virtue of going through the process. Nor do I believe that this is the intention of those who currently run the board. It was, after all, established in the first place to spare people the trauma of going through the courts. However, it is clear that the problems are significant. The RIRB must move to stop the hurt which has become so much part of the experience of the thousands of vulnerable people with whom it deals. It must also reappraise urgently the amounts it awards in the light of mounting evidence that it is now short-changing victims of abuse.

# Burying our heads in the sand
*May 3, 2007*

Almost exactly five years ago Deirdre de Barra publicly revealed the tragic personal circumstances which had afflicted herself and her family. It was an act of great bravery and was widely credited as a turning point in this country's tortured dealings with the issue of abortion. Deirdre wrote in a letter to this newspaper (February 25, 2002) that her unborn baby had recently been diagnosed with a severe chromosomal abnormality which would result in death soon after birth. At this stage she was 16 weeks pregnant. She made it clear that this was very much a wanted baby. But she added that "the trauma of this news was vastly exacerbated by the thought of being forced to carry to full term a foetus which would never know extra-uterine life".

The similarities between her experience and the dreadful situation in which Miss D currently finds herself should come as no surprise. While there is no statistical breakdown on the precise motivations of the roughly 6,000 Irish women who seek abortions in the UK each year, it is reasonable to consider that a number do so as a result of diagnosis of serious foetal abnormality. It is a cruel twist that having already received the devastating news that her baby will die at birth or shortly afterwards, a pregnant woman should then have to face the reality that there is no help for her in this country. All we tell her is that she must carry the pregnancy to term, regardless of her wishes. She can, of course, leave and take her problem elsewhere. We don't know anything about that, and we don't want to know. So long as the 6,000 remain anonymous and silent, the sand in which we collectively bury our heads remains comfortably undisturbed.

Every so often, though, reality intrudes, invariably in the form of the stark human suffering involved in such cases. So it is with Miss D's attempt this morning in the High Court to ensure that she will not be arrested and detained if she tries to leave the country to terminate her pregnancy. As we know her baby's brain defect will result in certain death almost immediately after birth. Deirdre de Barra's tragedy provided us with a similar insight five years ago. It had occurred in the maelstrom of the run-up to the fifth and latest referendum to amend the Constitution on abortion. This was the one where the Fianna Fáil-Progressive Democrats government of the day attempted to enshrine an entire piece of legislation in the Constitution.

Based on a commitment made in 1997, largely to placate a group of four Independent TDs on whom the then government relied for support, the proposal sought to remove a woman's right to an abortion in this country if she were at risk from suicide. This right had in turn arisen as a result of the X case in 1992, when the Supreme Court ruled that a suicidal 14-year-old girl, pregnant as a result of rape, was entitled to an abortion to safeguard her life. The 2002 referendum proposal was rejected by the electorate, as indeed had been a similar amendment put 10 years previously in the wake of the X case. Despite a particularly vitriolic campaign, full of dire predictions that a No vote would catapult us into abortion on demand, it was clear that there was no public will to impose draconian restrictions on women already facing such difficult choices in their lives.

However, none of the five abortion referendums so far has yet tackled the question of therapeutic abortion, where the foetus has severe abnormalities. The only official response to Deirdre de Barra's case in 2002 was a cryptic comment from the government that her situation was not "comprehended" by the proposed amendment to the Constitution.

Interestingly, however, it should be recalled that the three masters of the Dublin maternity hospitals, while supporting the 2002 referendum banning suicide as a reason for abortion, did agree that termination of pregnancy should be legally available in Ireland in cases such as Deirdre de Barra's. One of her main reasons in revealing her story was to point to the inhumanity involved in forcing her to "secretly seek contact numbers, book flights and accommodation, take trains and taxis to a strange hospital in a foreign city, to meet strange medical staff who see me as yet another statistic of the Irish problem, to be sent back to this country where there is no compassion - or else to carry on for a further five months, with all the attendant mental and physical strain, knowing that there will be a burial and not a baby to look forward to". She pleaded for legislation to address the issue. In the wake of the 2002 referendum, Bertie Ahern, Taoiseach then as now, said that it would be a matter for the next government - which is of course the one we've had for the past five years. Its refusal to act has been nothing short of craven.

# State failing children with autism
*May 10, 2007*

There is a group of families in this country who care little about how the Taoiseach bought his house, who gave him money or where he kept it. They deal daily with the reality that the State chooses to squander millions of euro fighting them in court rather than provide their children with a proper education. During the first five years of this century, the Department of Education spent at least €20 million on legal costs associated with defending its refusal to provide a specific type of education, Applied Behavioural Analysis (ABA) for children with autism.

Eoin Dempsey from Co Meath celebrated his seventh birthday yesterday. His family is one of many who are convinced that the State's approach to their autistic children's education is causing actual damage. As a result of a process of trial and error, Eoin's parents are now certain that their son desperately needs access to ABA. Their local GP and an independent psychologist agree wholeheartedly that Eoin urgently requires this kind of one-on-one educational therapy. The Department of Education, however, disagrees. All that is available for Eoin is a placement in a special unit attached to a mainstream national school. This is what Minister for Education Mary Hanafin calls the "eclectic" approach to catering for children with autism. But for Eoin, and for many hundreds of children like him, it simply did not work. He became severely distressed earlier this year when faced with the prospect of returning to school. He suffered a series of epileptic fits which were diagnosed as stress-related. His parents had previously managed to get him a few months of ABA treatment during the summer holidays, and Eoin had thrived. They were now confronted with a deeply unhappy little boy, who was deteriorating in front of their eyes as each day passed in his school placement. Gráinne Dempsey, Eoin's mother, is herself a primary school teacher. She could clearly see the system was failing her son and causing him acute misery because of his inability to deal with or even understand what was expected of him.

The tragedy of this kind of experience for many children with autism is that it can lock them into a pattern of profoundly disturbed behaviour, sometimes for life.
Eoin's parents have now withdrawn him from school on medical grounds. They are providing him with a home-based ABA programme and he is making excellent progress. Despite this, the Department of Education has refused to assist the family with funding. It is impossible to fathom why the State has such difficulty responding to the clear needs of families like the Dempseys. All they seek is an effective and appropriate education for their son. They tried what the department

told them would work. When it failed, the State simply turned its back on them. The Department of Education's hostility towards the provision of ABA for children with autism is equally inexplicable. The Government's own Task Force on Autism (2001) recommended its use. TCD lecturer Dr Rita Honan, a member of the Task Force, wrote last week to Taoiseach Bertie Ahern pointing out its findings that ABA was "by far superior to other approaches". In this context, she wrote, she was "continually stunned by the current Minister for Education's remarks that there is no 'preferred' method for teaching children with autism". She further recommended that the Taoiseach "respectfully advise the Minister for Education to personally familiarise herself with published reports and scientific literature, particularly around best practices for educating pre-school aged children with autism, rather than rely on information that is inaccurate, which is currently the case."

It is clear that the ignorance of both the Minister and her department is costing the taxpayer dearly. Even more seriously, though, it is condemning hundreds of children to a future which, as Rita Honan puts it, "denies the children their best chance at increasing their learning capacity, their IQ and future potential, and decreasing their autistic traits". The current election manifestos hold scant comfort for these children or their parents. Fianna Fáil and the PDs trot out meaningless platitudes supporting the provision of "appropriate" education for children with special needs. Autism is not even mentioned. Fine Gael is also disgracefully vague, with again no reference to ABA. Only two parties, Labour and the Greens, deal with the issue at all, both committing themselves to the provision of ABA for children who need it.

The image of Yvonne Ó Cuanacháin weeping outside the Four Courts last month remains vivid in the public mind. She and her husband had just lost the marathon legal case they had taken on behalf of their autistic six-year-old son Seán, to secure him ABA therapy. "The light of learning," Yvonne said at the time, "has been all but extinguished for Seán today." Come election day, voters should remember her words.

# Greens will need steel in spine
*May 31, 2007*

In the wake of the election result last week, the verdict of Green TD Paul Gogarty was that his party had been "too timid" in its campaign. It is a view that does not augur well for the kind of steel the Greens will need if they reach the point of serious negotiations with Fianna Fáil to form a coalition government.

The great potential strength of the Greens is that they do not have to be all things to all people. With a well-defined but narrow set of priorities, they can focus on a small number of specific issues and stick to them. Any talk of being a watchdog for Fianna Fáil would be disastrous. As the Progressive Democrats and indeed Labour before them discovered, this catapults a small coalition partner into an impenetrable moral morass, where you're damned whatever you do.

The Labour Party's support for the tax amnesty in 1993 was a classic example. Driven by Fianna Fáil, and outrageously advantageous to the disgracefully large cohort of wealthy people who had failed to pay their full share of tax over previous years, it ran contrary to everything that Labour stood for. And yet they swallowed it in the interests of stable government, and subsequently paid the price at the polls. How the Greens can avoid a similar fate will be a key dilemma for them. Their approach to it could be of great significance for the future of the country. With galloping climate change and rapidly rising bills to be paid under Kyoto to offset our carbon pollution, a strong Green voice urging tough environmental measures is of critical importance in identifying what will always be unpalatable choices. So far, the Greens have emphasised that environmental protection need not be at the expense of our prosperity or comfort. But in our hearts, we all know that there will come a time when sacrifices will have to be made, when our consumption of energy will have to be curtailed (by higher taxes, if necessary), when luxuries such as air travel and driving around in large, gas-guzzling cars will have to be drastically controlled. It is to a great extent the raison d'être for any Green Party to place these stark choices before us. If Green politicians become fatally undermined in this country by a brush with coalition, their message will be all too easy to ignore.

Last Sunday, Fianna Fáil's Dick Roche was at pains on the radio (Newstalk FM's The Wide Angle ) to argue that there really was very little difference between his party and the Greens on policy matters. And in some areas, this may well be true. It will be revealing over the coming weeks to observe precisely which aspects of its policies the Green Party will choose to emphasise - those closest to Fianna Fáil, or the radically divergent. In this context, it is worrying to see the Greens prioritise issues such as education and class sizes. Not that this is unimportant - far from it. But it is an area where agreement with Fianna Fáil would be relatively easy to secure, particularly as the latter have already promised to create 4,000 additional teaching posts. On the other hand, the Greens' pushing of the Kenny report's proposals to limit the price of development land will be far less popular with Fianna Fáil. Proper, controlled planning, rather than that which is driven by windfall profits to landowners, is a key plank in minimising energy and fuel use, and consequently appropriately central to the Greens' core environmental policies. The implementation of a carbon tax on fuel, a longstanding Green policy, is also anathema to Fianna Fáil. If the Greens stick to their guns on this one, and insist on a tax large enough to make us significantly change our profligate use of petrol and oil, they will have made significant inroads towards making us take our fair share of responsibility for limiting climate change.

In order to achieve any of this, there is much to be said for the Greens' clarity of thought about ethics in politics and in particular their espousal of a ban on corporate donations to political parties.

For as long as politics is funded by those whose business interests will be most damaged by real and significant environmental control, we will see no major change. The Greens' strategy to alter fundamentally the entire basis of how politics is paid for would certainly be a lasting contribution to public life in this country. All of this, however, presupposes that Fianna Fáil is willing to pay the price of coalition with the Greens, and indeed that the Green Party is prepared to demand a high enough price. Political parties with long experience of coalition become masters at fudging issues. Novices may not even perceive a fudge until it is too late. Or even worse, they may get their fudges in first, compromising frantically all the way up the aisle in order to make it to the altar.

# Canada's familiar abuse tale
*June 21, 2007*

At lunchtime today President Mary McAleese is in Canada to perform the official opening of Ireland Park, a memorial to the 38,000 Irish famine victims who emigrated to Toronto in 1847. These Irish were part of a wave of white settlers who pushed westwards in Canada during the 19th century, exiles from their own land in turn exiling the original inhabitants, the Indians or First Nations peoples, from theirs.

Exile, however, is by no means all we had in common. As I discovered last weekend, we shared an almost identical approach to particular groups of children, whom we locked up and generally starved, beat, raped and abused for much of the 20th century. I was in Calgary (in central Canada) at the invitation of Phil Fontaine, national chief of the General Assembly of First Nations, to address a major conference on the Truth and Reconciliation Commission in the process of being established to deal with the legacy of the Canadian Indian residential schools. The Canadians were curious about the Irish industrial schools and had asked me to explain what had happened in this country, both historically and more recently as we attempted to come to terms with our own record of savagery towards institutionalised children.

In Canada during the latter half of the 19th century, as white settlers pushed the native peoples from their land, the Canadian government resolved on a final settlement of what it called the "Indian problem". Indians would be assimilated, "civilised" and "tamed". They would be trained to become useful members of Canadian society, filling suitably menial positions of labourers and servants. The plan to eliminate entire cultures, a kind of cultural genocide, would start with the children. Virtually all First Nations youngsters - boys and girls - were forcibly removed from their families and dispatched often hundreds of miles away to residential schools. Once there, they were taken apart and broken, with the stated aim of turning them into good little English, or French-speaking, Christians. In an uncanny echo of the Irish industrial schools, the Canadian government decided to hand the management over to religious. Catholic religious orders ran two-thirds of the 130 schools, with the remainder managed by Anglicans, Methodists and Presbyterians. Most prominent among the Catholic religious orders who ran the schools were the Oblates of Mary Immaculate, whom of course we know well in this country as having presided with such unapologetic brutality over the reformatory for boys in Daingean, Co Offaly. This was the place where the Oblate in charge informed a visiting delegation in the late 1960s, in the most matter-of-fact manner, that he favoured the beating of children naked, as this was more humiliating for them.

Appalling abuses were also routine throughout the 100-year history of the Indian residential schools in Canada, the last of which closed in 1996; 150,000 native children are estimated to have gone through the system, exactly the same number as here in Ireland. About 80,000 survivors of the Canadian system are alive today - in this country it is reckoned at about 30,000. In all, three generations of First Nations, Métis and Inuit children had their culture, language and religion literally beaten out of them. Gruesome punishments were devised for children as young as five caught speaking their own languages, with accounts of pins being hammered through their tongues. The effects of such extensive brutality, combined with widespread sexual abuse and the endless years of being told that they and their parents and families were evil and worthless, have left Canadian native communities severely damaged, but not defeated.

Amid a plethora of court cases and class actions, the Canadian government finally agreed a settlement with First Nations negotiators last year. There is to be a central reparations scheme, which will compensate all those forced to attend residential schools, with higher amounts for those who were physically or sexually abused.
The Truth and Reconciliation Commission, also part of the settlement, was chosen as a mechanism where survivors could feel safe telling their stories. It is a key tenet that the process for revealing the truth should in no way result in further harm to the survivors. This is a principle which we seem to have lost sight of. The reports of hurt, humiliation and upset emerging from the Residential Institutions Redress Board are disturbingly numerous. The drastic reduction in the number of cases being investigated by the Ryan Child Abuse Commission has left many survivors confused and angry. Both of these processes have been surrounded by a level of secrecy which can only be described as obsessive. As the Canadians embark on their own dark but necessary journey into their cruel and criminal past, they could learn from our experience that processes which started out with the best of intentions have ended up doing perhaps as much harm as good to those who suffered the most as children.

# Hospital's gripe does not wash

*June 28, 2007*

It was one of the better examples of how appearances can deceive. Last week, it emerged that the Health Service Executive underspent its capital budget by almost €100 million, and now has to give the money back. On the same day, it was reported that the National Maternity Hospital (in Holles Street, Dublin) had been turned down by the HSE for additional funding to enable it to clean its facility more thoroughly. Clearly another example of HSE incompetence, one might think, in this instance potentially endangering babies and their mothers by refusing essential funding to clean a busy maternity hospital, while at the same time handing money back because it was incapable of spending it on a health service which remains chronically underfunded. However, while there is little excuse for the HSE's underspend, things are not quite as clear when it comes to Holles Street. The hospital was commendably frank in its recently published annual report for 2006 on its cleaning problems, particularly about the "urgent need" for more frequent cleaning. As everyone is now well aware of the connection between dirty hospitals and life-threatening infections, the allocation of sufficient funding to hygiene should be a key priority for all health facilities. In the case of Holles Street, however, there are other items of major expenditure that it is not quite so frank about. These concern the substantial legal costs of its battle to keep secret some of the records relating to the retention by the hospital of the organs of deceased babies.

Holles Street was one of the more active hospitals in terms of retaining babies' organs after postmortem examination, invariably without either the consent or the knowledge of the infants' parents. These parents, through the organisation Parents For Justice, sought the release of the relevant documentation from all the maternity and paediatric hospitals involved in this practice throughout the State. All but one eventually capitulated. Holles Street not only refused, but then took a High Court action against the Information Commissioner, who had ruled that the Holles Street records be released under the Freedom of Information Act. The documents in question relate to the material sent by Holles Street to the Dunne inquiry, which had been established to examine the entire issue of organ retention, and which was closed down by the government in 2005 without publishing a full report. In the absence of such a report, the parents are attempting to piece together exactly what the various hospitals told the inquiry. In the case of Holles Street, according to its legal representatives, these records contain "highly confidential and sensitive information [providing] information on post mortem practices and procedures".

# Hospital's gripe does not wash

Two months ago, the High Court dismissed the appeal by Holles Street against the decision of the Information Commissioner that the records be released. It found against the hospital on all six grounds quoted and ruled that the Information Commissioner had been correct in each instance. The hospital had 28 days from the date of this judgment to release the records to Parents For Justice. This deadline ran out weeks ago, and still no documents have been handed over. In addition, Holles Street refuses to say how much the legal action has cost the hospital. It will have to pay the costs of the other side in addition to its own. At a rough and highly conservative estimate, these will amount to at least €250,000 - a figure which would buy quite a lot of cleaning materials. Holles Street receives most of its funding from the taxpayer, through the HSE. The State, however, does not own the hospital and it remains unclear what, if any, sanctions can be applied in the context of a hospital spending exchequer funds on futile legal battles rather than on, for instance, cleanliness and infection control. In terms of the hospital's governance, it is worth noting that the 2006 annual report for Holles Street informs us that of the six ex-officio members of the hospital's board of governors, no fewer than four are Roman Catholic priests.

The expenditure by Holles Street on its legal battles was firmly criticised by the Information Commissioner, Emily O'Reilly. In her 2004 annual report, she wrote that "the behaviour of the Hospital in this case amounted to obstruction of my Office ... In conducting its business with my Office in this manner, the Hospital is likely to have incurred substantial and mostly unnecessary legal costs which ultimately must be at the expense of the taxpayer." Meanwhile, in the cleanliness stakes, Holles Street is the dirtiest of the three large Dublin maternity hospitals. Although it did improve last year, its record on general cleanliness in wards, toilets and kitchens, and on hand hygiene in some areas, remains in the "poor" category. The attempt by Holles Street to blame the HSE and its refusal to release funds for this simply will not wash.

# THE RYAN REPORT

# Report a monument to a society's shame
*May 21, 2009*

**OPINION:** *IT IS quite simply a devastating report. It is a monument to the shameful nature of Irish society throughout most of the decades of the 20th century, and arguably even today, writes* **MARY RAFTERY**

Mr Justice Seán Ryan and the child abuse commission have produced a work of incalculable value to this country. They have painstakingly charted the vast scale of abuse of tens of thousands of children within institutions. Crucially, they have ascribed responsibility for that abuse by examining the role and reactions of the authorities concerned – the twin pillars of church and State which colluded so disastrously in the misery of so many children.

Irish society has a long record of running away from the appalling truth of the physical and sexual torture experienced by so many children across over 100 childcare institutions. Many have found a myriad of ways to remain in denial.

Just a few bad apples, they say. And it's all in the past anyway. Most disgraceful have been the snide suggestions that those revealing their abuse are motivated by compensation rather than the truth. These are the excuses which have been peddled by the religious orders, most notably the Christian Brothers, over the decades. The Ryan commission report makes clear that it has been a deliberate strategy by this and other orders to deny, to obfuscate and to challenge any and all of the allegations against them. What is so important is that it is not merely a historic failing on their part – it remains their approach to this day. Only a single religious order is singled out as having a more open and accepting approach to both the inquiry process and to the victims themselves – this is the Institute of Charity, known as the Rosminian order, who ran viciously abusive schools at Ferryhouse in Clonmel and Upton in Cork and who now seek to understand how their ideals could have become so debased.

While some of the other religious orders, and indeed the State, have made public apologies, these are of highly questionable value in the face of the continuing attempts by both church and State to evade responsibility and intimidate victims. The Ryan report is particularly interesting on this particular form of hypocrisy. On the public apology by the Christian Brothers, it says it was "guarded, conditional and unclear", and that "it was not even clear that the statement could properly be called an apology".

Crucially, the abject failure by most of the congregations to accept any responsibility for the abuse has been identified repeatedly by the commission. In this respect, its findings are targeted directly at the current leadership within these organisations.

Again in the case of the Christian Brothers, the report draws a pointed distinction between the evidence of contrition given by many individual Brothers who had worked in the industrial schools, and the attitude of blanket denial coming from those who are currently in charge of the congregation.

The commission describes a range of problems encountered when dealing with the Christian Brothers: assertions "known to be incorrect or misleading"; relevant facts omitted; and a policy of denying that a Brother was ever in an institution where "a complainant had got a name even slightly wrong".

It should be remembered that many of the religious congregations implicated in the abuse continue to run hundreds of primary and secondary schools across Ireland today.

The Christian Brothers remain the largest provider of schools for boys, while the Sisters of Mercy provide the same facility for girls. Another savagely abusive congregation – the Brothers of Charity, whose abuse of mentally handicapped boys is catalogued in the report's chapter on its institution at Lota in Cork – continues today to be the largest provider of care facilities for both adults and children with intellectual disabilities.

This asks important questions of us as a society: are we simply to sweep this under the carpet, to conveniently agree that everything is much better today? Or should we instead look to change a system where so much of the educational and care provision for our children is farmed out to organisations who are unaccountable and now proven to have a long track record of abuse and cover-up?

And what of the State and the Department of Education? They too stand condemned for their abject and grotesque failures to protect the children in their care. Grossly inadequate inspection and regulation, combined with wilfully turning a blind eye when complaints were made are detailed repeatedly in the commission's report.

And again, we perceive a pattern where this is no mere failing of a past era. We know that the Department of Education is currently fighting child sex abuse victims in the courts to ensure that the State is declared to have no legal responsibility for what happened to them. The State has even gone so far as to threaten victims that it will force them to pay its own legal costs (as well as theirs) should they continue to attempt to hold the State to account. This kind of bullying, threatening behaviour is redolent of the attitudes which the Ryan commission report describes as pervasive in the 1940s and 1950s. Nonetheless, hundreds of victims of child sexual abuse by day-school teachers continue today to experience what can fairly be described as a campaign of State-sponsored intimidation in their attempts to seek justice in the courts.

We have heard all about the ordeal of Louise O'Keeffe, terrified that she might lose her house to pay the State's legal bills on foot of her case against the Department of Education over sexual abuse by her school principal, which she suffered at the age of eight.

A number of cases concerning another primary school teacher, the notorious former Christian Brother Donal Dunne, are similarly being fought by the State. This sexual predator is the subject of an entire chapter in the Ryan commission report, which also included day-school abuse within its remit.

It is an account of staggering negligence on the part of every single element of the educational system involved. Dunne (referred to as John Brander in the report) moved blithely from school to school across the midlands, sexually assaulting children in each of them, despite detailed knowledge at senior government and Catholic Church levels that he was a paedophile.

It should be pointed out that the report has some failings, most particularly the decision not even to name perpetrators of abuse who have been criminally convicted. It is difficult to fathom the rationale for this, and it is likely to lead to a certain understandable frustration from victims.

Further, the report's recommendations are disappointingly vague and brief, and do not do justice to the meticulous attention to detail and the plain, frank language of the main body of the report.

In particular, there are two key issues which are not addressed. In the face of such an avalanche of abuse of highly vulnerable children, the question of a specific constitutional provision for the protection of the rights of children should become central to any debate flowing from this report. It is painfully clear that the general protections for children as part of a family unit were pitifully inadequate to save these tens of thousands of children from abuse in times past, and seem similarly incapable today. A recommendation in this area would have been helpful.

Secondly, there is the issue of mandatory reporting of child abuse. This has been a highly controversial area, with strenuous opposition from various professional groups responsible for child welfare. A White Paper on the issue, promised by the then taoiseach Bertie Ahern when he made his historic apology to child abuse victims in 1999, failed to materialise. It remains up to any individual as to whether information about a child at risk is passed on to the appropriate authorities.

The Ryan report is a testament to what happens when discretion prevails. While there has undoubtedly been enormous progress in child protection mechanisms since the days of the industrial schools, we do know that children at risk continue to be let down by the State, remaining in abusive conditions without protection. At the very least, it would have been useful for the child abuse commission to have again raised the reporting issue for debate.

However, what the Ryan commission report has done with great thoroughness is to give us a compelling vision of the hell to which so many children were consigned. It is up to ourselves as a society to demand from Government a series of guarantees, constitutional in part, to ensure that it is never again repeated.

# Taxpayers pick up the bill while abusers get secrecy and protection

*May 22, 2009*

**OPINION:** *The deal making religious orders liable for a mere fraction of the cost of the abuse of children in their care underlines the vulnerability of a State owning so little of its vital social infrastructure, writes* **MARY RAFTERY**

DID YOU know that you and I, as taxpayers, have actually paid to keep secret the identities of the abusers referred to in the Ryan commission report? That's in addition, of course, to footing over 90 per cent of the estimated €1.3 billion cost to compensate victims of abuse through the Residential Institutions Redress Board. It is one of the many bitter ironies to emerge during the past decade of inquiry into the abuse of children in over 100 institutions in this country. When protecting their own (usually financial) interests, the religious orders displayed a zeal and even ferocity notably absent from their attempts down the years to control the criminal battery, assault and rape perpetrated by their member Brothers, priests and nuns against small children.

The trick of making us pay to maintain the confidentiality of known child abusers was a particularly good wheeze. It unfolded as follows: the Christian Brothers took the child abuse commission to court, seeking that it be prohibited from naming any Brothers it found responsible for abuse. Many were dead or infirm, it was argued, and could no longer defend themselves. Further, the point was made that this might also mean a prohibition on naming the institutions concerned, as it could lead to discovery of the identities of the relevant perpetrators. While the Brothers did not win their High Court case, they did force more stringent investigative procedures on to the commission. They then proceeded to lodge an appeal to the Supreme Court, and only dropped their case having extracted from the commission a commitment that it would itself take the decision not to name anyone responsible for abuse. As Justice Seán Ryan stated in 2004, it would have been fatal to the commission had it also been precluded from naming specific institutions.

And who paid for all this legal posturing which resulted in such secrecy and protection for abusers? Not the Christian Brothers. They won their costs in court, and the entire bill was born by the child abuse commission – which of course means you and I, the taxpayers. When it comes to the cost of the redress scheme for abuse victims, it is now painfully obvious that we have been the victims of an enormous con. At the time of the notorious Church-State deal, capping the contribution of the religious orders at €128 million (and only a fraction of that in hard cash), the religious orders claimed there had been no cover-up of abuse and no protection of abusers. We now discover from the Ryan report that this was a lie, and that several religious orders not only knew all about the abusers in their midst but concealed that knowledge from the rest of us.

Nonetheless, we heard repeated statements from government ministers (most notably Bertie Ahern and Charlie McCreevy) about the good work of the religious congregations, about how we should be grateful to them and how it would be wrong to bankrupt them. This in spite of the fact that the religious orders were never asked by the State for their accounts, and had been busily squirreling away huge sums through the sale of swathes of their valuable land banks at the height of the property boom. This appalling deal, worth hundreds of millions to the orders who shielded (and continue to protect) child abusers, was finalised in such a way as to hide it as much as possible from public scrutiny.

The main architect of the deal was minister for education Michael Woods and, wouldn't you know it, he and his cute cabinet colleagues rubber stamped it on June 5th, 2002 – the very last day of the outgoing Fianna Fáil/PD coalition government. Ministers paid it scant heed – their attention, like the rest of the country's – was firmly fixed on the Ireland v Germany World Cup match. They adjourned early that day to get to the nearest television set. It subsequently emerged that both Department of Finance officials and the attorney general's office were unhappy with how the deal had come to pass. Both had been excluded from much of the negotiation, which, unusually, was handled by Woods and his secretary general John Dennehy alone. It was generally felt by State officials that a 50/50 split of the redress cost between the State and the religious orders was the fairest option. An equal sharing of the responsibility for the abuse of so many thousands of children was considered entirely appropriate. The religious orders, however, were not biting. Take it or leave it, they said – not a penny more than €128 million. In return, they were getting a full indemnity from the State for all future court cases taken against them by those who had suffered at their hands.

Only yesterday, Minister for Children Barry Andrews stated twice on RTÉ Radio One's News At One that the government had no power to compel religious orders to contribute anything at all to the redress fund. The deal was the best the State could do at the time. This is at best a highly disingenuous view of the past. Compulsion never arose. It was a matter of a simple trade – the State had something to sell, namely a valuable indemnity, and the religious orders were keen to buy. That the latter managed to secure full State protection through the indemnity at such a knockdown price is to the eternal shame of every single member of that cabinet in 2002. There was speculation at the time that there were other issues informing what was so clearly such an abysmal deal for the taxpayer. In particular, there had been anxiety around the issue of ownership of a number of key hospitals in the country – notably St Vincent's, belonging to the Sisters of Charity, and the Mater, belonging to the Sisters of Mercy.

Health administrators had received a nasty shock some years previously when the Medical Missionaries of Mary had hinted that they might sell the Our Lady of Lourdes Hospital in Drogheda to a private consortium. As a key hospital for the northeast, this would have had a disastrous impact on the public health service for the region. It was with relief that the nuns eventually sold to the local health board, ensuring that the hospital was transferred into public hands. The fear that the Sisters of Mercy and Charity – both implicated in the running of seriously abusive institutions for children – might decide to raise funds through the sale to private interests of their major Dublin hospitals was thought likely to have informed some of the thinking behind the notorious deal. What this underlines is the vulnerability of a State which owns and controls so little of its vital social infrastructure. For as long as several of our key hospitals, and the majority of our schools, remain in the possession of religious orders, we will continue to be vulnerable to the naked self-interest of nuns, priests and Brothers who have now been so thoroughly discredited by the Ryan report.

# THE MURPHY REPORT

# Bishops lied and covered up
*November 27, 2009*

*The report shows that what lies at the heart of the Catholic Church in Ireland is a profound and widespread corruption, perpetrated by liars, child sex abusers and those at the very top who covered up their crimes, writes* **MARY RAFTERY**

THERE IS one searing, indelible image to be found in the pages of the Dublin diocesan report on clerical child abuse. It is of Fr Noel Reynolds, who admitted sexually abusing dozens of children, towering over a small girl as he brutally inserts an object into her vagina and then her back passage. That object is his crucifix.

The report details how this man was left as parish priest of Glendalough (and in charge of the local primary school) for almost three years after parents had complained about him to former archbishop of Dublin Desmond Connell during the 1990s. In 1997, he was finally moved and appointed as chaplain to the National Rehabilitation Hospital in Dún Laoghaire. The report helpfully informs us that there were 94 children aged 18 or under as inpatients here. The hospital authorities were told nothing of Reynolds's past or of suspicions that he was a child abuser. This kind of callous disregard for the safety of children is found over and over again in the report. Bishops lied, cheated and covered up, almost as a matter of course, in a display of relentless cynicism spanning decades. Children were blithely sacrificed to protect priests, the institution and its assets. It is, consequently, difficult to avoid the conclusion that what lies at the heart of the Catholic Church (at least in Ireland) is a profound and widespread corruption.

The Dublin report divides the bulk of its analysis into chapters devoted to individual priest abusers. But reading through the stomach-churning details of their crimes, another parallel reality appears. Behind almost each one of these paedophiles was at least one bishop (often more) who knew of the abuse, but failed to protect children. Some of them, Pontius Pilate-like, washed their hands, merely reporting it up the line. Others actively protected the criminals in their midst by destroying files and withholding information. Their handling of complaints is variously described as "particularly bad", "disastrous" and "catastrophic".

Dermot Ryan stands out as the most callous of the Dublin archbishops. He failed properly to investigate complaints against at least six of the worst offending priests. Kevin McNamara was little better, but his tenure was considerably briefer, limiting some of the damage he did. John Charles McQuaid is severely criticised in one case, but it was not within the commission's remit to examine his reign in any significant detail. His response to the pornographic photos of two children taken by one of his priests is a damning indictment of the impact of priestly celibacy. He viewed the criminal act as an expression of "wonderment" by the priest at the nature of the female body.

And what of Desmond Connell, perhaps the most reviled of them all? A complex picture emerges of a man unsuited to the task facing him, attempting to deal with the enormous scale of abuse in the archdiocese, and ultimately failing. While he did, for instance, engage with the civil authorities, unlike his predecessors, he, nonetheless, continued to maintain secrecy over much of what the diocese knew of their child-abusing priests.

As for the many Dublin auxiliary bishops, two stand out as being particularly awful. There is arguably enough evidence in this report to send bishops James Kavanagh (now deceased) and Dermot O'Mahony (retired) to prison for failing to report crimes. Or at least, there would be if there existed such an offence. Incredibly, there is none. We certainly used to have one; called misprision of felony, it was conveniently dropped from the statute books in 1998 when the felony laws changed. The effect was that no priest, bishop, or indeed lay person, could be charged with failing to report criminal activity of which they were aware. What a sigh of relief the bishops of Ireland must have breathed. The report describes Bishop O'Mahony's involvement in the cases of 13 priests from its sample of 46 under investigation. It mentions that he was aware of allegations against several more. His cover-up over his 21 years in office was extensive.

Bishop Kavanagh directly attempted to pervert the course of justice by seeking to influence one Garda investigation and by convincing a family to drop a complaint against another priest. He appears at various stages in a number of other cases, always failing to act to protect children. Bishop Donal Murray of Limerick is also indicted as having handled a number of complaints badly. He will have very serious questions to answer over the coming days. Recently retired bishop of Ossory Laurence Forristal equally stands condemned, which is all the more egregious as he was in charge of the archdiocese's efforts during the 1990s to respond to the crisis and draw up child protection guidelines. Bishops James Moriarty of Kildare and Leighlin, retired Bishop Brendan Comiskey and Auxiliary Bishop of Dublin Éamonn Walsh also all knew of complaints of abuse at various stages.

A week before the broadcast in 2002 of RTÉ television's Prime Time Cardinal Secrets (which led to the establishment of the Dublin commission), Cardinal Connell engaged in a pre-emptive strike. He had refused to appear on the programme. He chose instead to circulate each of his 200 parishes with a letter read out at every Mass that Sunday. In it, he apologised for the failures of the past, but blamed them on a lack of understanding within the church of paedophilia. The commission is categorical in its refusal to accept this plea of ignorance as an excuse. It refers bluntly to the inconsistency between such claims and the decision in 1986 to take out an insurance policy to protect church assets from abuse victims. At that time, we are told that the archdiocese knew of allegations of child sex abuse against 20 of its priests. The report further notes the documented history of the church's detailed awareness of paedophilia as both crime and sin spanning the past 2,000 years. The first reference dates from AD 153.

Finally, the report refers to the fact that Archbishop Ryan displayed as early as 1981 a complete understanding of both the recidivist nature of paedophilia and of the devastating damage it caused to child victims. There had been a consistent denial from church authorities that anyone knew anything about either of these key factors until very recently. Perhaps most damning of all is the report's findings as to the general body of priests in Dublin. While it gives credit to a small few who courageously pursued complaints, it adds that "the vast majority simply chose to turn a blind eye". What emerges most clearly from the report is that priests, bishops, archbishops and cardinals had the greatest difficulty in telling right from wrong, and crucially that their determination of what constituted wrongdoing was vastly different from that of the population at large. This fact is worthy of reflection on the part of all those who remain connected to the church through its continuing and often central involvement in the provision of services such as education and health throughout the country.

In 2003, ex-governor of Oklahoma Frank Keating drew parallels between the behaviour of some US Catholic bishops and the Cosa Nostra. It drew a storm of protest, and he resigned from his position as chairman of the church-appointed oversight committee on child abuse. However, it is not too far-fetched a comparison to the Irish church in the light of the three investigations into its behaviour we have had to date. The organised, premeditated pattern of secrecy and concealment of crime is worthy of the world's most notorious criminal fraternity.

# Every auxiliary bishop had some knowledge of crimes

*December 3, 2009*

**ANALYSIS:** *It's not just about Bishop Donal Murray. Many other bishops failed and they should all resign, writes* **MARY RAFTERY**

AS BISHOP Donal Murray thrashes about trying to save his own skin, it is clear he is doing immense damage to his brother bishops, as he divides and sets them against each other. It is not too difficult to find a rationale for his tenacity in the face of such strong public revulsion at his lack of action to protect children from gruesome abuse – he was not the only one (true), and consequently it is unfair that he be singled out to pay for the gross negligence of so many other bishops (also true). The answer to this is not of course that Donal Murray should remain as bishop of Limerick. It is rather that all the other guilty ones should also resign. The point has been made that some of these are more seriously implicated than others, and all should not be tarred with the same brush. However, this is to miss the single most crucial aspect underlying all of this – namely that each and every auxiliary bishop in Dublin had some knowledge of heinous crimes against children and did not perform their duty as citizens to report this knowledge of criminal activity to the Garda. This is what at heart defines the cover-up. The reason we know that each of them had such knowledge is that the Dublin report tells us that the auxiliary bishops met regularly, once a month, and that at these meetings they discussed cases of specific priests who were known to have sexually abused children.

Ten of the bishops involved in this cover-up are still alive. Five remain in office and five are retired. The focus quite properly is on those who continue to exercise the functions of bishop, particularly as this involves such an extensive controlling interest in schools. Three former auxiliaries are now full bishops. First among these is Donal Murray, whose tenure spanned the reigns of three archbishops – Ryan, McNamara and Connell.

The details of Bishop Murray's callous lack of action in at least three cases of clerical child abusers are by now well known. He has in his own defence chosen to emphasise that he had been a bishop for only 18 months when approached by the two men in Valleymount who voiced complaints about Fr Thomas Naughton being "too close to the altar boys". His lack of proper action, he claims, was due to his inexperience. It is of interest to note that Bishop Murray was no obscure curate when elevated to auxiliary bishop in 1982. He was no less than professor of moral theology at Clonliffe College, the capital's main seminary. Further, he was expert on ethics, in which subject he lectured extensively in UCD.

Next up is Jim Moriarty, bishop of Kildare and Leighlin, who was an auxiliary in Dublin from 1991 to 2002. This is the key period during which there was an explosion in the number of complaints of clerical child sex abuse in Dublin. Consequently, the subject would have arisen repeatedly at the monthly meetings of auxiliaries during this period, adding to the knowledge of crime which each of them was covering up. We also know he received a very specific complaint about Fr Edmondus, the priest who abused Marie Collins (among others) at Our Lady's children's hospital in Crumlin. His response was to pass it up the line to his archbishop and wash his hands of it. In a statement last Sunday to his parishes in Kildare, he made no reference to this. He, like his fellow bishops, focused on the crimes of the abusing priests while conveniently ignoring their own heartless and cynical betrayal of children through their cover-up.

Then there is Martin Drennan, bishop of Galway. He is barely mentioned in the report. However, as auxiliary bishop in the capital from 1997 to 2005, he must share in the complicity over cover-up. Although he had no responsibility for the earlier periods during the 1980s and 1990s when cover-up was routine and automatic, he nonetheless functioned during a period when the archdiocese considered itself under no obligation to co-operate with Garda investigations and continued to hide information of criminal acts from the civil authorities.

Of those who remain auxiliary bishops in Dublin, the most interesting is Éamonn Walsh He is tipped as successor to Archbishop Diarmuid Martin, and is deeply immersed in the politics of the Dublin archdiocese. An auxiliary since 1990, he was intimately acquainted with diocesan secrets even before that in his capacity as secretary to the archbishop from 1985. Previously, he had been head of Clonliffe College since 1977. Given his longevity at the heart of the Dublin archdiocese, Eamonn Walsh perhaps more than most of his fellow bishops faces the charge of cover-up and failure to report his knowledge of crime to the civil authorities.

Finally, there is Raymond Field. An auxiliary since 1997, he is a barrister, having been called to both the Irish and the English bar, and so should have been acutely aware of the overriding duty to report all knowledge of crime to the police. There is no evidence that he did so. Further, he is directly criticised in the Dublin report. With regard to the case of Fr Benito, Bishop Field did not convey complete information to a parish priest with regard to serious concerns around this priest's relations with certain children. This was as recently as 2003.

The retired bishops who must also stand condemned as central to the cover-up are Cardinal Desmond Connell, bishops Laurence Forristal, Dermot O'Mahony, Brendan Comiskey and Fiachra Ó Ceallaigh. Worst among these are Connell and O'Mahony, although Comiskey and Forristal are also singled out for stern criticism by the Murphy commission. Of all 10 of these surviving Dublin bishops, only a single one (Forristal) admitted "unequivocally" to the commission that he had handled complaints badly. This gives some sense of the moral bankruptcy that permeates the ranks of the supposed moral and religious leaders of our society.

# Index

*Compiled by Róisín Nic Cóil*

Index

Index

Index

# Index

# Index

Letterfrack industrial school 115–16
Levi, Primo 115
Limerick Regional Hospital 23–4
Livingstone, Ken 11
Logan, Emily 95
London, 4x4 vehicles 11
Lota, Cork 153
Lovett, Anne 37
Lynch, Tom 9
McAleese, Mary 87–8, 147
McCall, Ian 60
McCartan, Ron 139–40
McCarthy, Dermot 21
McCole, Brigid 135
McConville, Jean 32
McCreevy, Charlie 11–12, 41–2, 157
McDowell, Michael 17–18, 44, 95, 110, 123–4
McGinty, Brendan 85–6
McGuinness, Breffni 86
McGuinness, Catherine 96
McGuire, Martin 10
McInerney, Maud 25
McLaughlin, Mitchel 32
McNamara, Archbishop Kevin 160, 163
McQuaid, John Charles 160–1
McSharry, Andy "Bull" 59, 77–8
Madonna House 132
Magdalens 3–4, 84
Mahon-Smith, Walter 10
Manweiler, John 51
Mara, PJ 97
Martin, Archbishop, Dr Diarmuid 75
        successor tipped 164
Martin, Judge Mary 30
Martin, Micheál 2, 33, 56
Mater hospital 73, 121–2, 158
Meany, Paul 76
Mearsheimer, Prof John 102

Index

Index

Residential Institutions Redress Board (RIRB) 40, 139–40, 148, 156
Reynolds, Fr Noel 160
Riefenstahl, Leni 98
Robinson, Mary 79
Roche, Dick 145
Rooney, Paul 77
Rooskey, Co Roscommon 17–18
Rosminian Order 151
RTÉ 15–16, 87, 97–8
Russell, Seán 32
Ryanair 85–6, 113–14
Ryan, Archbishop Dermot 160–2, 163–4
Ryan report 151–8
Ryan, Mr Justice Seán 151, 152, 156
St Joseph's, Kilkenny 39–40
St Patrick's Institution 124
St Paul insurance company 1–2
St Vincent's hospital 73, 157–8
Shannon, Geoffrey 95–6
Sheehy-Skeffington, Owen 115
Shortall, Paddy 92
Shucksmith, Prof Mark 63–4
Sinn Féin 32
SIPTU 42
Sisters of Charity, Irish 139–40
        St Vincent's hospital 73, 157–8
Sisters of Mercy 122, 153, 157–8
Sisters of Our Lady of Charity of Refuge 3–4
Slattery Communications 121–2
Sligo General Hospital 55–6
Smyth, Mr Justice Thomas 113–14
Social and Family Affairs, Department of 8
Social Services Inspectorate 105–6
Stokes, Chris 107
Sustainable Energy Ireland 65–6
Tallon, Bernie, Bernard and Michelle 119–20
Tangermann, Stevan 69
Teagasc 48, 63–4

# Index